50 Celebrity Chef Recipes for Home

By: Kelly Johnson

Table of Contents

- Gordon Ramsay - Beef Wellington
- Jamie Oliver - Chicken Tikka Masala
- Nigella Lawson - Chocolate Cake
- Bobby Flay - Grilled BBQ Ribs
- Ina Garten - Roast Chicken
- Anthony Bourdain - Boeuf Bourguignon
- Rachael Ray - Spaghetti Carbonara
- Giada De Laurentiis - Lasagna
- Emeril Lagasse - Shrimp Étouffée
- Wolfgang Puck - Pizza Margherita
- Julia Child - Beef Bourguignon
- Martha Stewart - Lemon Bars
- Alton Brown - Roast Turkey
- Guy Fieri - Cajun Shrimp Pasta
- Padma Lakshmi - Chicken Curry
- Heston Blumenthal - Perfect Steak
- Mario Batali - Risotto
- Paula Deen - Southern Fried Chicken
- Mary Berry - Victoria Sponge Cake
- David Chang - Ramen
- Bobby Flay - Fish Tacos
- Rachel Khoo - Croissants
- Marcus Samuelsson - Jerk Chicken
- Yotam Ottolenghi - Mediterranean Salad
- Thomas Keller - Beef Short Ribs
- Carla Hall - Biscuits and Gravy
- Alex Guarnaschelli - Beef Stroganoff
- Jose Andres - Paella
- Ainsley Harriott - Jamaican Jerk Chicken
- Rick Bayless - Guacamole
- Gino D'Acampo - Tiramisu
- Anne Burrell - Spaghetti and Meatballs
- Curtis Stone - Grilled Steak
- Nancy Silverton - Artisan Bread
- Lidia Bastianich - Gnocchi

- Hugh Fearnley-Whittingstall - Roast Pork Belly
- Sanjeev Kapoor - Butter Chicken
- Cat Cora - Greek Salad
- Lorraine Pascale - Chocolate Brownies
- David Chang - Korean BBQ
- Jamie Oliver - Prawn Linguine
- Marcus Wareing - Beef Wellington
- Yotam Ottolenghi - Shakshuka
- Eric Ripert - Bouillabaisse
- Gail Simmons - Apple Pie
- Dominique Ansel - Cronuts
- Carla Hall - Fried Chicken
- Julia Child - Coq au Vin
- Wolfgang Puck - Pumpkin Soup
- Ina Garten - Lemon Roast Chicken

Gordon Ramsay - Beef Wellington

Ingredients:

- 1 ½ lb (700g) beef fillet
- Salt and freshly ground black pepper
- Olive oil
- 1 tbsp English mustard
- 7 oz (200g) mushrooms, finely chopped
- 1 tbsp fresh thyme leaves
- 2-3 slices of Parma ham or prosciutto
- 10 oz (300g) puff pastry
- 1 egg yolk, beaten (for egg wash)

Instructions:

1. Prepare the Beef:
    - Season the beef fillet generously with salt and pepper.
    - Heat a frying pan with a little olive oil until very hot. Sear the beef fillet all over until nicely browned. Remove from the pan and set aside to cool.
2. Prepare the Mushroom Duxelles:
    - In the same pan, add a little more olive oil if needed and sauté the chopped mushrooms with thyme until they release their moisture and become golden brown. Season with salt and pepper. Remove from heat and let cool.
3. Assemble the Wellington:
    - Spread a thin layer of English mustard over the cooled beef fillet.
    - Lay out a large sheet of plastic wrap and arrange the slices of Parma ham or prosciutto in an overlapping layer to form a rectangle large enough to wrap around the beef.
    - Spread the mushroom duxelles evenly over the ham.
4. Wrap the Beef:
    - Place the seared beef fillet in the center of the ham and mushroom layer. Using the plastic wrap, carefully roll the ham and mushroom mixture around the beef, shaping it into a tight log. Twist the ends of the plastic wrap to secure. Refrigerate for at least 20 minutes to firm up.
5. Prepare the Pastry:
    - Roll out the puff pastry on a floured surface to a rectangle large enough to wrap the beef completely.
6. Assemble and Bake:
    - Remove the plastic wrap from the beef. Place the beef in the center of the rolled-out puff pastry.
    - Brush the edges of the pastry with beaten egg yolk.
    - Carefully fold the pastry over the beef, sealing all the edges tightly. Trim any excess pastry if necessary.

        - Place the Wellington seam side down on a baking sheet lined with parchment paper.
        - Brush the entire pastry with egg wash for a golden finish.
7. Bake:
        - Preheat the oven to 400°F (200°C).
        - Bake the Beef Wellington for 20-25 minutes until the pastry is golden brown and cooked through.
        - Remove from the oven and let it rest for 10 minutes before slicing.
8. Serve:
        - Slice the Beef Wellington into thick slices and serve with your choice of sides, such as roasted vegetables and mashed potatoes.

Enjoy your homemade Gordon Ramsay-style Beef Wellington!

Jamie Oliver - Chicken Tikka Masala

Ingredients:

- 4 skinless, boneless chicken breasts
- Salt and freshly ground black pepper
- 1 lemon
- 1 large bunch of fresh cilantro (coriander), leaves picked, stalks finely chopped
- 2 cloves of garlic, peeled and finely chopped
- 1 thumb-sized piece of fresh ginger, peeled and finely chopped
- 2 fresh red chilies, deseeded and finely chopped
- Olive oil
- 2 teaspoons ground cumin
- 2 teaspoons ground paprika
- 2 teaspoons ground turmeric
- 2 teaspoons garam masala
- 2 tablespoons tomato purée
- 1 x 14 oz (400g) can of chopped tomatoes
- 1 x 14 oz (400ml) can of coconut milk
- Basmati rice, to serve

Instructions:

1. Marinate the Chicken:
    - Cut the chicken breasts into bite-sized chunks and season with salt and pepper.
    - In a bowl, combine the juice of half the lemon with half the cilantro stalks, half the garlic, half the ginger, half the chili, and a tablespoon of olive oil. Add the chicken pieces and toss to coat. Cover and refrigerate for at least 1 hour (or overnight for deeper flavor).
2. Make the Tikka Masala Sauce:
    - Heat a large pan over medium heat and add a splash of olive oil.
    - Add the remaining garlic, ginger, chili, and cilantro stalks to the pan. Cook for 5 minutes until softened.
    - Stir in the ground cumin, paprika, turmeric, and garam masala. Cook for another 2 minutes until fragrant.
    - Add the tomato purée, chopped tomatoes, and coconut milk. Bring to a simmer, then reduce the heat and cook gently for 15 minutes, stirring occasionally.
3. Cook the Chicken:
    - While the sauce is simmering, preheat the grill (broiler) to high.
    - Thread the marinated chicken pieces onto skewers and grill for 10-12 minutes, turning occasionally, until cooked through and charred in places.
4. Finish the Dish:

- Remove the chicken from the skewers and add it to the sauce. Stir gently to combine and simmer for a further 5 minutes until the chicken is heated through and coated in the sauce.
- Taste and season with salt, pepper, and a squeeze of lemon juice if needed.
5. Serve:
    - Sprinkle the remaining cilantro leaves over the Chicken Tikka Masala and serve hot with basmati rice.

Enjoy your homemade Jamie Oliver-style Chicken Tikka Masala! Adjust the spice levels to your preference by adding more or less chili.

Nigella Lawson - Chocolate Cake

Ingredients:

For the cake:

- 1 3/4 cups (225g) all-purpose flour
- 1 1/2 cups (300g) granulated sugar
- 1/2 cup (50g) cocoa powder
- 1 1/2 teaspoons baking powder
- 1 1/2 teaspoons baking soda
- 2 large eggs
- 1/2 cup (120ml) whole milk
- 1/2 cup (120ml) vegetable oil
- 2 teaspoons vanilla extract
- 1 cup (240ml) boiling water

For the frosting:

- 1/2 cup (120g) unsalted butter, softened
- 1 cup (120g) powdered sugar (icing sugar)
- 1/4 cup (30g) cocoa powder
- 1 teaspoon vanilla extract
- 2-3 tablespoons whole milk

Instructions:

1. Preheat and Prepare:
    - Preheat your oven to 350°F (180°C). Grease and line two 8-inch (20cm) round cake pans with parchment paper.
2. Make the Cake Batter:
    - In a large mixing bowl, sift together the flour, sugar, cocoa powder, baking powder, and baking soda.
    - In another bowl, whisk together the eggs, milk, vegetable oil, and vanilla extract.
    - Gradually add the wet ingredients to the dry ingredients, mixing until smooth and well combined.
    - Carefully stir in the boiling water, a little at a time, until the batter is smooth. The batter will be quite liquid, but that's normal.
3. Bake the Cakes:
    - Divide the batter evenly between the prepared cake pans.
    - Bake in the preheated oven for 25-30 minutes, or until a toothpick inserted into the center of the cakes comes out clean.
    - Remove from the oven and allow the cakes to cool in the pans for 10 minutes before turning them out onto a wire rack to cool completely.
4. Make the Frosting:

- In a mixing bowl, beat the softened butter until creamy.
- Gradually sift in the powdered sugar and cocoa powder, beating well after each addition.
- Add the vanilla extract and 2 tablespoons of milk, then beat the frosting until smooth and fluffy. If needed, add an additional tablespoon of milk to achieve a spreadable consistency.

5. Assemble the Cake:
    - Once the cakes are completely cool, place one cake layer on a serving plate or cake stand.
    - Spread a generous layer of frosting over the top of the first cake layer.
    - Place the second cake layer on top and spread the remaining frosting evenly over the top and sides of the cake.
6. Decorate and Serve:
    - Optionally, decorate the cake with chocolate shavings, sprinkles, or additional cocoa powder.
    - Slice and serve your delicious Nigella Lawson-style chocolate cake!

This recipe delivers a moist and rich chocolate cake that's sure to impress any chocolate lover. Enjoy baking!

Bobby Flay - Grilled BBQ Ribs

Ingredients:

For the ribs:

- 2 racks of pork baby back ribs (about 3-4 pounds total)
- Salt and freshly ground black pepper

For the dry rub:

- 1/4 cup brown sugar
- 2 tablespoons smoked paprika
- 2 tablespoons chili powder
- 1 tablespoon garlic powder
- 1 tablespoon onion powder
- 1 tablespoon ground cumin
- 1 tablespoon ground coriander
- 1 tablespoon kosher salt
- 1 tablespoon freshly ground black pepper

For the BBQ sauce:

- 1 cup your favorite BBQ sauce (store-bought or homemade)
- 1/4 cup apple cider vinegar
- 2 tablespoons honey
- 1 tablespoon Dijon mustard
- 1 tablespoon Worcestershire sauce
- 1 teaspoon hot sauce (optional, adjust to taste)

Instructions:

1. Prepare the Ribs:
   - Remove the membrane from the back of the ribs if it's still attached. Use a small knife to loosen it, then grip it with a paper towel and pull it off.
   - Season the ribs generously with salt and pepper on both sides.
2. Make the Dry Rub:
   - In a small bowl, combine all the dry rub ingredients: brown sugar, smoked paprika, chili powder, garlic powder, onion powder, ground cumin, ground coriander, salt, and pepper. Mix well.
3. Rub the Ribs:
   - Sprinkle the dry rub evenly over both sides of the ribs, patting it in to adhere. You may not need to use all of the rub; use enough to coat the ribs well.
4. Prepare the BBQ Sauce:

- In a saucepan, combine the BBQ sauce, apple cider vinegar, honey, Dijon mustard, Worcestershire sauce, and hot sauce (if using). Bring to a simmer over medium heat, then reduce the heat and let it simmer gently for 5-10 minutes, stirring occasionally, until slightly thickened. Remove from heat.
5. Grill the Ribs:
    - Preheat your grill to medium-high heat (about 300-350°F or 150-175°C).
    - Place the ribs on the grill, bone-side down, and cook with the lid closed for about 30 minutes.
6. Apply BBQ Sauce:
    - Brush the top side of the ribs generously with the prepared BBQ sauce. Close the lid and continue to grill for another 30 minutes.
7. Flip and Repeat:
    - Flip the ribs over so they are meat-side down. Brush the bone-side with more BBQ sauce. Close the lid and grill for 15-20 minutes.
8. Final Glazing:
    - Flip the ribs once more so they are meat-side up. Brush with a final layer of BBQ sauce and grill for another 15-20 minutes, or until the ribs are tender and caramelized, and the internal temperature reaches about 200°F (93°C).
9. Rest and Serve:
    - Remove the ribs from the grill and let them rest for 5-10 minutes before slicing between the bones and serving.

Enjoy Bobby Flay's flavorful grilled BBQ ribs with your favorite sides like coleslaw, cornbread, or grilled vegetables. It's a perfect dish for a summer barbecue or any occasion you want to impress with delicious ribs!

Ina Garten - Roast Chicken

Ingredients:

- 1 (4 to 5 pounds) whole chicken, preferably organic
- Kosher salt and freshly ground black pepper
- 1 large bunch of fresh thyme, plus a few sprigs for stuffing the chicken
- 1 lemon, halved
- 1 head of garlic, cut in half crosswise
- 2 tablespoons unsalted butter, melted
- 1 large yellow onion, thickly sliced
- Olive oil

Instructions:

1. Preheat the Oven:
    - Preheat your oven to 425°F (220°C).
2. Prepare the Chicken:
    - Remove any giblets from the chicken cavity and pat the chicken dry with paper towels. This helps the skin crisp up nicely.
    - Liberally season the inside of the chicken with salt and pepper. Stuff the cavity with the bunch of thyme, lemon halves, and garlic halves.
3. Truss the Chicken (Optional):
    - Trussing is optional but can help the chicken cook more evenly. Using kitchen twine, tie the legs together and tuck the wing tips under the body of the chicken.
4. Prepare the Pan:
    - In a large roasting pan, toss the onion slices with a little olive oil and scatter them across the bottom of the pan. This will elevate the chicken slightly and add flavor to the drippings.
5. Roast the Chicken:
    - Place the chicken on top of the onions in the roasting pan. Brush the melted butter all over the chicken. Drizzle with a little olive oil and sprinkle generously with salt and pepper.
6. Roast:
    - Roast the chicken in the preheated oven for 1 1/2 hours to 1 hour and 45 minutes, or until the juices run clear when you cut between a leg and thigh.
7. Rest and Serve:
    - Remove the chicken from the oven and let it rest for 15 minutes on a cutting board with a rimmed plate tented loosely with aluminum foil before carving.
8. Carve and Enjoy:
    - Carve the chicken into slices and serve with the roasted onions and any pan juices poured over the top.

Ina Garten's roast chicken is beautifully simple yet flavorful, making it a perfect meal for any occasion, from casual dinners to special gatherings.

Anthony Bourdain - Boeuf Bourguignon

Ingredients:

- 2 pounds (900g) beef chuck, cut into 1-inch cubes
- Salt and freshly ground black pepper
- 2 tablespoons olive oil
- 4 ounces (120g) pancetta or thick-cut bacon, diced
- 2 medium carrots, peeled and sliced
- 1 medium onion, chopped
- 2 cloves garlic, minced
- 1 tablespoon tomato paste
- 1/4 cup (60ml) brandy or cognac
- 1 bottle (750ml) red wine (Burgundy or Pinot Noir)
- 2 cups (480ml) beef broth
- 1 bouquet garni (a bundle of fresh thyme, parsley, and a bay leaf tied together with kitchen twine)
- 1 pound (450g) small potatoes, halved or quartered
- 1/2 pound (225g) pearl onions, peeled
- 1/2 pound (225g) mushrooms, quartered
- Chopped fresh parsley, for garnish

Instructions:

1. Preheat and Prepare:
    - Preheat your oven to 325°F (160°C).
2. Brown the Beef:
    - Season the beef cubes generously with salt and pepper.
    - Heat the olive oil in a large Dutch oven or heavy-bottomed pot over medium-high heat. Add the beef cubes in batches and brown them on all sides. Transfer the browned beef to a plate and set aside.
3. Cook the Pancetta and Vegetables:
    - In the same pot, add the diced pancetta or bacon and cook until browned and crispy. Remove with a slotted spoon and set aside.
    - Add the sliced carrots and chopped onion to the pot and cook until softened, about 5 minutes. Add the minced garlic and cook for another minute until fragrant.
4. Deglaze and Simmer:
    - Stir in the tomato paste and cook for 1-2 minutes to caramelize slightly.
    - Pour in the brandy or cognac, stirring to scrape up any browned bits from the bottom of the pot.
    - Return the beef and pancetta/bacon to the pot. Pour in the red wine and beef broth. Add the bouquet garni. Bring to a simmer.
5. Braise in the Oven:

- Cover the pot with a lid and transfer it to the preheated oven. Braise for 2 to 2 1/2 hours, or until the beef is tender and can be easily pierced with a fork.
6. Add Potatoes, Pearl Onions, and Mushrooms:
    - About 30 minutes before the end of cooking, add the halved or quartered potatoes, pearl onions, and quartered mushrooms to the pot. Continue cooking until the vegetables are tender.
7. Serve:
    - Remove the bouquet garni from the pot. Taste and adjust seasoning with salt and pepper if needed.
    - Serve the Boeuf Bourguignon hot, garnished with chopped fresh parsley.

Anthony Bourdain's Boeuf Bourguignon is rich, comforting, and perfect served with crusty bread or over mashed potatoes to soak up the delicious sauce. Enjoy this hearty French classic!

Rachael Ray - Spaghetti Carbonara

Ingredients:

- 1 pound (450g) spaghetti
- 1/2 pound (225g) pancetta or guanciale, diced
- 2 tablespoons extra-virgin olive oil
- 4 cloves garlic, minced
- 3 large eggs
- 1 cup (100g) grated Parmesan cheese, plus extra for serving
- Salt and freshly ground black pepper
- Fresh parsley, chopped (optional, for garnish)

Instructions:

1. Cook the Spaghetti:
    - Cook the spaghetti in a large pot of salted boiling water according to package instructions until al dente. Reserve 1 cup of pasta cooking water, then drain the spaghetti.
2. Cook the Pancetta/Guanciale:
    - While the spaghetti is cooking, heat the olive oil in a large skillet over medium heat. Add the diced pancetta or guanciale and cook until crispy and browned, about 5-7 minutes. Add the minced garlic and cook for another 1-2 minutes until fragrant. Remove from heat.
3. Prepare the Sauce:
    - In a large mixing bowl, whisk together the eggs and grated Parmesan cheese until well combined.
4. Combine Everything:
    - Add the hot drained spaghetti to the skillet with the pancetta/guanciale and toss well to combine. The heat from the pasta will cook the eggs slightly and create a creamy sauce. If the mixture seems dry, add some of the reserved pasta cooking water a little at a time until desired consistency is reached.
5. Season and Serve:
    - Season the spaghetti carbonara with salt and freshly ground black pepper to taste.
    - Serve immediately, garnished with extra grated Parmesan cheese and chopped fresh parsley if desired.

Rachael Ray's spaghetti carbonara is a quick and satisfying dish, perfect for a weeknight dinner or anytime you're craving a comforting pasta meal. Enjoy!

Giada De Laurentiis - Lasagna

Ingredients:

For the Meat Sauce:

- 1 tablespoon olive oil
- 1 onion, finely chopped
- 3 cloves garlic, minced
- 1 pound (450g) ground beef or Italian sausage
- 1 teaspoon dried oregano
- 1 teaspoon dried basil
- 1/2 teaspoon salt, or to taste
- 1/4 teaspoon freshly ground black pepper, or to taste
- 1 can (28 ounces) crushed tomatoes
- 1/4 cup chopped fresh basil leaves

For the Lasagna:

- 1 pound (450g) lasagna noodles, cooked according to package instructions
- 15 ounces (425g) ricotta cheese
- 1 cup (100g) grated Parmesan cheese, plus extra for sprinkling on top
- 1 large egg
- 1/4 cup chopped fresh parsley leaves
- 1/2 teaspoon salt
- 1/4 teaspoon freshly ground black pepper
- 3 cups (300g) shredded mozzarella cheese

Instructions:

1. Make the Meat Sauce:
   - In a large skillet or saucepan, heat the olive oil over medium-high heat. Add the chopped onion and cook until softened, about 5 minutes.
   - Add the minced garlic and cook for another 1-2 minutes until fragrant.
   - Add the ground beef or Italian sausage to the skillet, breaking it up with a spoon. Cook until browned and cooked through, about 5-7 minutes.
   - Stir in the dried oregano, dried basil, salt, and pepper. Add the crushed tomatoes and bring to a simmer. Reduce the heat to low and let it simmer for 15-20 minutes, stirring occasionally, until the sauce has thickened slightly. Stir in the chopped fresh basil. Remove from heat and set aside.
2. Prepare the Lasagna Noodles:
   - Cook the lasagna noodles according to package instructions until al dente. Drain and set aside. Toss with a little olive oil to prevent sticking.
3. Make the Cheese Mixture:

- In a medium bowl, combine the ricotta cheese, grated Parmesan cheese, egg, chopped parsley, salt, and pepper. Mix well until smooth and well combined.
4. Assemble the Lasagna:
    - Preheat your oven to 375°F (190°C).
    - Spread a thin layer of the meat sauce on the bottom of a 9x13-inch baking dish.
    - Arrange a layer of cooked lasagna noodles over the sauce, overlapping slightly.
    - Spread half of the ricotta cheese mixture evenly over the noodles.
    - Sprinkle with 1 cup of shredded mozzarella cheese.
    - Spoon half of the remaining meat sauce over the cheese layer.
    - Repeat layers: noodles, ricotta mixture, mozzarella cheese, and meat sauce.
    - Finish with a final layer of noodles topped with the remaining meat sauce. Sprinkle generously with the remaining shredded mozzarella cheese and grated Parmesan cheese.
5. Bake the Lasagna:
    - Cover the baking dish loosely with aluminum foil. Bake in the preheated oven for 45 minutes.
    - Remove the foil and bake for an additional 10-15 minutes, or until the cheese is melted and bubbly and the edges are golden brown.
6. Rest and Serve:
    - Let the lasagna rest for 10-15 minutes before slicing and serving.
    - Garnish with additional chopped fresh basil or parsley, if desired.

Giada De Laurentiis' lasagna is a comforting and hearty dish, perfect for feeding a crowd or enjoying leftovers. It's a classic Italian-American favorite that's sure to please everyone at the table!

Emeril Lagasse - Shrimp Étouffée

Ingredients:

- 1/2 cup (1 stick) unsalted butter
- 1/2 cup all-purpose flour
- 1 large onion, finely chopped
- 1 bell pepper, finely chopped
- 2 celery ribs, finely chopped
- 3 cloves garlic, minced
- 1 teaspoon salt, or to taste
- 1/2 teaspoon cayenne pepper, or to taste
- 1/2 teaspoon smoked paprika
- 1/2 teaspoon dried thyme
- 1/4 teaspoon freshly ground black pepper
- 2 cups seafood or chicken broth
- 1 pound (450g) shrimp, peeled and deveined
- 2 tablespoons chopped fresh parsley, plus extra for garnish
- Cooked white rice, for serving

Instructions:

1. Make the Roux:
    - In a large Dutch oven or heavy-bottomed pot, melt the butter over medium heat. Add the flour and stir constantly to make a roux. Cook the roux, stirring frequently, until it turns a deep golden brown color, similar to the color of peanut butter, about 15-20 minutes. Be careful not to burn it.
2. Sauté the Vegetables:
    - Add the chopped onion, bell pepper, and celery to the pot with the roux. Cook, stirring occasionally, until the vegetables are softened, about 5-7 minutes.
    - Add the minced garlic, salt, cayenne pepper, smoked paprika, dried thyme, and black pepper. Cook for another 1-2 minutes until fragrant.
3. Add Broth and Simmer:
    - Gradually pour in the seafood or chicken broth, stirring constantly to incorporate into the roux and vegetables. Bring to a simmer and cook for 10-15 minutes, stirring occasionally, until the mixture thickens slightly.
4. Add Shrimp and Parsley:
    - Add the peeled and deveined shrimp to the pot. Cook for 5-7 minutes, or until the shrimp are pink and cooked through.
5. Serve:
    - Stir in the chopped fresh parsley.
    - Serve the shrimp étouffée hot over cooked white rice.
    - Garnish with additional chopped parsley, if desired.

Emeril Lagasse's shrimp étouffée is rich in flavor with a perfect blend of spices, making it a delicious and satisfying dish. Enjoy this Cajun classic with family and friends!

Wolfgang Puck - Pizza Margherita

Ingredients:

For the Pizza Dough:

- 1 pound (450g) pizza dough, store-bought or homemade
- Cornmeal or flour, for dusting

For the Pizza Toppings:

- 1/2 cup tomato sauce or pizza sauce
- 8 ounces (225g) fresh mozzarella cheese, sliced or torn into pieces
- 1-2 ripe tomatoes, thinly sliced
- Fresh basil leaves, torn or chopped
- Extra-virgin olive oil
- Salt and freshly ground black pepper, to taste

Instructions:

1. Preheat the Oven:
    - Preheat your oven to the highest temperature possible, typically around 500°F (260°C), with a pizza stone or baking sheet inside if using.
2. Prepare the Pizza Dough:
    - On a lightly floured surface, roll out the pizza dough into a round shape, about 12 inches (30cm) in diameter. Alternatively, you can shape it by hand for a rustic look.
3. Assemble the Pizza:
    - Sprinkle cornmeal or flour on a pizza peel or the back of a baking sheet.
    - Place the rolled-out pizza dough on the prepared surface.
    - Spread the tomato sauce evenly over the dough, leaving a small border around the edges for the crust.
    - Arrange the sliced fresh mozzarella cheese evenly over the sauce.
    - Place the thinly sliced tomatoes on top of the cheese.
    - Season with salt and freshly ground black pepper to taste.
    - Drizzle a little extra-virgin olive oil over the pizza.
4. Bake the Pizza:
    - Carefully transfer the assembled pizza onto the preheated pizza stone or baking sheet in the oven.
    - Bake for about 10-12 minutes, or until the crust is golden brown and the cheese is bubbly and slightly browned.
5. Finish and Serve:
    - Remove the pizza from the oven and immediately sprinkle with torn or chopped fresh basil leaves.
    - Drizzle with a bit more extra-virgin olive oil if desired.

- Slice and serve hot.

Wolfgang Puck's Pizza Margherita celebrates the simplicity of fresh ingredients and the delicious combination of flavors. It's perfect for a casual dinner or a gathering with friends. Enjoy your homemade pizza!

Julia Child - Beef Bourguignon

Ingredients:

- 3 pounds (1.5 kg) beef chuck roast, cut into 2-inch cubes
- Salt and freshly ground black pepper
- 3 tablespoons olive oil
- 3 tablespoons all-purpose flour
- 1 onion, finely chopped
- 2 carrots, peeled and sliced
- 4 cloves garlic, minced
- 1 bottle (750 ml) red wine, preferably Burgundy or Pinot Noir
- 2 cups (480 ml) beef broth
- 2 tablespoons tomato paste
- 1 bouquet garni (a bundle of fresh thyme, parsley, and a bay leaf tied together with kitchen twine)
- 8 ounces (225 g) pearl onions, peeled
- 8 ounces (225 g) mushrooms, quartered
- Chopped fresh parsley, for garnish

Instructions:

1. Preheat and Prepare:
   - Preheat your oven to 325°F (160°C).
2. Season and Brown the Beef:
   - Pat the beef cubes dry with paper towels and season generously with salt and pepper.
   - In a large Dutch oven or heavy-bottomed pot, heat 2 tablespoons of olive oil over medium-high heat. Working in batches, add the beef cubes and brown them on all sides. Transfer the browned beef to a plate and set aside.
3. Cook the Vegetables:
   - In the same pot, add the remaining 1 tablespoon of olive oil. Add the chopped onion and sliced carrots. Cook for about 5 minutes, stirring occasionally, until softened.
   - Add the minced garlic and cook for another minute until fragrant.
4. Deglaze and Simmer:
   - Sprinkle the flour over the vegetables and stir to coat evenly. Cook for 1-2 minutes to cook out the raw flour taste.
   - Slowly pour in the red wine, stirring constantly to scrape up any browned bits from the bottom of the pot.
   - Add the beef broth, tomato paste, and bouquet garni. Stir to combine.
5. Braise in the Oven:
   - Return the browned beef cubes (and any accumulated juices) to the pot. Bring the mixture to a simmer.

- Cover the pot with a lid and transfer it to the preheated oven. Braise for 2 1/2 to 3 hours, or until the beef is tender and can be easily pierced with a fork.
6. Prepare the Pearl Onions and Mushrooms:
    - While the beef is braising, prepare the pearl onions and mushrooms.
    - In a separate skillet, heat a tablespoon of olive oil over medium heat. Add the pearl onions and cook until they start to brown, about 5-7 minutes.
    - Add the quartered mushrooms and cook for another 5 minutes until they are tender and lightly browned. Set aside.
7. Finish the Dish:
    - Once the beef is tender, remove the pot from the oven. Discard the bouquet garni.
    - Stir in the cooked pearl onions and mushrooms.
    - Taste and adjust seasoning with salt and pepper if needed.
8. Serve:
    - Ladle the Beef Bourguignon into bowls or onto plates. Garnish with chopped fresh parsley.
    - Serve hot, ideally with crusty bread, mashed potatoes, or over egg noodles.

Julia Child's Beef Bourguignon is a labor of love, rich in flavor and perfect for special occasions or a comforting meal. Enjoy the hearty and delicious taste of this iconic French dish!

Martha Stewart - Lemon Bars

Ingredients:

For the crust:

- 1 cup (2 sticks or 225g) unsalted butter, softened
- 1/2 cup (100g) granulated sugar
- 2 cups (250g) all-purpose flour
- 1/4 teaspoon salt

For the lemon filling:

- 1 1/2 cups (300g) granulated sugar
- 1/4 cup (30g) all-purpose flour
- 4 large eggs
- 2/3 cup (160ml) fresh lemon juice (from about 4-5 lemons)
- Zest of 2 lemons (optional, for extra lemon flavor)
- Powdered sugar, for dusting

Instructions:

1. Preheat and Prepare:
   - Preheat your oven to 350°F (175°C). Grease a 9x13-inch baking pan or line it with parchment paper, leaving an overhang on the sides for easy removal.
2. Make the crust:
   - In a mixing bowl, cream together the softened butter and granulated sugar until light and fluffy.
   - Add the flour and salt to the butter mixture and mix until combined and crumbly.
   - Press the mixture evenly into the bottom of the prepared baking pan.
3. Bake the crust:
   - Bake in the preheated oven for 20-25 minutes, or until the crust is lightly golden brown. Remove from the oven and set aside.
4. Make the lemon filling:
   - In another bowl, whisk together the granulated sugar and flour.
   - Whisk in the eggs, lemon juice, and lemon zest (if using) until smooth and well combined.
5. Assemble and bake:
   - Pour the lemon filling over the warm crust, spreading it evenly.
   - Return the pan to the oven and bake for 25-30 minutes, or until the filling is set and the edges are lightly golden brown.
6. Cool and serve:
   - Allow the lemon bars to cool completely in the pan on a wire rack.
   - Once cooled, dust the top with powdered sugar.

- Use the parchment paper overhang to lift the bars out of the pan and onto a cutting board.
- Cut into squares or bars.

Martha Stewart's Lemon Bars are refreshingly tart and sweet, with a buttery crust that complements the tangy lemon filling perfectly. They're ideal for picnics, parties, or a delightful dessert any time of year. Enjoy these bright and zesty treats!

Alton Brown - Roast Turkey

Ingredients:

- 1 whole turkey (12-14 pounds)
- Salt and freshly ground black pepper
- 1 onion, quartered
- 1 lemon, quartered
- 1 head of garlic, halved crosswise
- Several sprigs of fresh herbs (such as thyme, rosemary, and sage)
- 1/2 cup (1 stick) unsalted butter, melted
- Chicken or turkey broth, for basting

Instructions:

1. Preparation:
   - Preheat your oven to 325°F (165°C).
2. Prepare the Turkey:
   - Remove the giblets and neck from the turkey cavity (reserve for making gravy if desired).
   - Rinse the turkey inside and out with cold water, then pat dry with paper towels.
   - Season the cavity generously with salt and pepper.
   - Stuff the cavity with the quartered onion, lemon, garlic, and fresh herbs.
3. Truss the Turkey (Optional):
   - Trussing the turkey helps it cook more evenly and keeps the stuffing in place. Use kitchen twine to tie the legs together and tuck the wing tips under the bird.
4. Season and Roast:
   - Place the turkey breast side up on a rack in a roasting pan.
   - Brush the melted butter all over the turkey, making sure to coat it evenly.
   - Season the outside generously with salt and pepper.
5. Roasting:
   - Roast the turkey in the preheated oven. Plan for about 15 minutes of cooking time per pound of turkey, but use a meat thermometer to ensure it reaches an internal temperature of 165°F (74°C) in the thickest part of the thigh without touching bone.
6. Basting:
   - Every 30 minutes, baste the turkey with the pan juices or chicken/turkey broth to keep it moist and flavorful.
7. Resting and Carving:
   - Once the turkey reaches the desired temperature, remove it from the oven and tent loosely with foil.
   - Let the turkey rest for at least 20-30 minutes before carving to allow the juices to redistribute.
8. Serve:

- - Carve the turkey and serve with your favorite side dishes and gravy.

Alton Brown's roast turkey recipe ensures a beautifully golden and juicy bird with minimal fuss, perfect for Thanksgiving or any festive occasion. Enjoy the delicious results!

Guy Fieri - Cajun Shrimp Pasta

Ingredients:

- 1 pound (450g) shrimp, peeled and deveined
- Cajun seasoning (store-bought or homemade)
- 8 ounces (225g) linguine or fettuccine pasta
- 2 tablespoons olive oil
- 1 tablespoon unsalted butter
- 1 bell pepper, thinly sliced (any color you prefer)
- 1 onion, thinly sliced
- 3 cloves garlic, minced
- 1 cup (240ml) chicken broth
- 1 cup (240ml) heavy cream
- Salt and freshly ground black pepper, to taste
- Fresh parsley, chopped (for garnish)
- Grated Parmesan cheese, for serving

Cajun Seasoning (if making homemade):

- 1 tablespoon paprika
- 1 tablespoon garlic powder
- 1 tablespoon onion powder
- 1 tablespoon dried oregano
- 1 tablespoon dried thyme
- 1 teaspoon cayenne pepper (adjust to taste)
- 1 teaspoon salt
- 1 teaspoon black pepper

Instructions:

1. **Prepare the Shrimp:**
   - Pat the shrimp dry with paper towels and season generously with Cajun seasoning. Set aside.
2. **Cook the Pasta:**
   - Cook the pasta in a large pot of salted boiling water according to package instructions until al dente. Drain and set aside.
3. **Sauté the Vegetables:**
   - In a large skillet, heat olive oil and butter over medium-high heat.
   - Add the bell pepper and onion slices. Cook for 3-4 minutes until softened.
4. **Cook the Shrimp:**
   - Push the vegetables to the side of the skillet and add the seasoned shrimp in a single layer. Cook for 1-2 minutes per side until pink and cooked through.
   - Add the minced garlic and cook for another 1 minute until fragrant.

5. Make the Sauce:
   - Pour in the chicken broth and heavy cream. Stir to combine and bring to a simmer.
   - Season with salt and pepper to taste. Let it simmer for 2-3 minutes until slightly thickened.
6. Combine Pasta and Sauce:
   - Add the cooked pasta to the skillet with the shrimp and sauce. Toss everything together until well coated and heated through.
7. Serve:
   - Remove from heat and garnish with chopped fresh parsley.
   - Serve the Cajun shrimp pasta hot, sprinkled with grated Parmesan cheese.

Guy Fieri's Cajun Shrimp Pasta is a flavorful and satisfying dish that brings together the richness of cream, the heat of Cajun seasoning, and the freshness of shrimp. It's perfect for a quick and delicious dinner any day of the week!

Padma Lakshmi - Chicken Curry

Ingredients:

- 1 1/2 pounds (680g) boneless, skinless chicken thighs or breasts, cut into bite-sized pieces
- Salt and freshly ground black pepper
- 2 tablespoons vegetable oil or ghee
- 1 large onion, finely chopped
- 3 cloves garlic, minced
- 1-inch piece of ginger, peeled and minced
- 1 tablespoon curry powder
- 1 teaspoon ground turmeric
- 1 teaspoon ground cumin
- 1 teaspoon ground coriander
- 1/2 teaspoon cayenne pepper (adjust to taste)
- 1 can (14 ounces) diced tomatoes
- 1 can (14 ounces) coconut milk
- 1 cup (240ml) chicken broth or water
- Juice of 1/2 lemon or lime
- Fresh cilantro leaves, chopped (for garnish)
- Cooked rice or naan, for serving

Instructions:

1. Season and Sear the Chicken:
    - Season the chicken pieces with salt and pepper.
    - Heat the vegetable oil or ghee in a large skillet or Dutch oven over medium-high heat. Add the chicken pieces in batches and sear until browned on all sides. Remove the chicken from the skillet and set aside.
2. Sauté the Aromatics:
    - In the same skillet, add the chopped onion and cook until softened and translucent, about 5 minutes.
    - Add the minced garlic and ginger, and cook for another 1-2 minutes until fragrant.
3. Add Spices:
    - Stir in the curry powder, ground turmeric, ground cumin, ground coriander, and cayenne pepper. Cook for 1 minute to toast the spices, stirring constantly.
4. Simmer the Curry:
    - Add the diced tomatoes (with their juices) to the skillet. Stir to combine and cook for 2-3 minutes.
    - Pour in the coconut milk and chicken broth or water. Bring the mixture to a simmer.
5. Cook the Chicken:

- Return the seared chicken pieces to the skillet along with any juices that have accumulated. Stir to coat the chicken in the curry sauce.
- Reduce the heat to medium-low, cover the skillet, and let the curry simmer for 20-25 minutes, stirring occasionally, until the chicken is cooked through and tender.
6. Finish and Serve:
    - Stir in the lemon or lime juice. Taste and adjust seasoning with salt and pepper if needed.
    - Garnish with chopped fresh cilantro leaves.
    - Serve the chicken curry hot over cooked rice or with naan bread.

Padma Lakshmi's Chicken Curry is rich, flavorful, and aromatic, perfect for enjoying with family and friends. It captures the essence of Indian cuisine with its warm spices and creamy coconut milk base. Enjoy this comforting dish as a delicious meal!

Heston Blumenthal - Perfect Steak

Ingredients:

- 2 thick-cut steaks (such as ribeye, New York strip, or filet mignon), about 1-1.5 inches thick
- Salt and freshly ground black pepper
- Olive oil or clarified butter
- Optional: Garlic cloves, fresh thyme, and/or rosemary for extra flavor

Instructions:

1. Preparation:
   - Remove the steaks from the refrigerator about 30 minutes before cooking to bring them to room temperature. This ensures more even cooking.
2. Season the Steaks:
   - Pat the steaks dry with paper towels to remove any excess moisture.
   - Season both sides of the steaks generously with salt and freshly ground black pepper. Let them sit for a few minutes to allow the seasoning to penetrate.
3. Preheat the Pan:
   - Heat a heavy-bottomed skillet (preferably cast iron) over medium-high to high heat. You want the pan to be very hot to achieve a good sear on the steak.
4. Cooking the Steaks:
   - Drizzle a little olive oil or clarified butter into the hot pan. Swirl the pan to coat the bottom evenly.
   - Carefully place the seasoned steaks in the hot pan. Cook without moving them for about 2-3 minutes, depending on the thickness of the steak and desired doneness for medium-rare.
   - If using, add garlic cloves, fresh thyme, or rosemary to the pan for extra flavor.
5. Searing and Browning:
   - After 2-3 minutes, flip the steaks using tongs. Cook for another 2-3 minutes for medium-rare, or adjust the time according to your preferred doneness.
   - During this time, you can baste the steaks with the melted butter or oil in the pan to enhance flavor and moisture.
6. Resting:
   - Once the steaks are cooked to your liking, remove them from the pan and transfer them to a plate. Let them rest for 5-10 minutes. This allows the juices to redistribute throughout the meat, ensuring a juicy steak.
7. Serve:
   - Slice the steaks against the grain and serve immediately while still hot.

Heston Blumenthal emphasizes the importance of resting the steak after cooking to achieve the perfect texture and juiciness. This method ensures a beautifully seared exterior with a tender, juicy interior. Enjoy your perfectly cooked steak with your favorite sides and sauces!

Mario Batali - Risotto

Ingredients:

- 1 1/2 cups Arborio rice (or Carnaroli rice)
- 4 cups chicken or vegetable broth (homemade or low-sodium store-bought)
- 1/2 cup dry white wine
- 1 small onion, finely chopped
- 2 cloves garlic, minced
- 2 tablespoons unsalted butter
- 2 tablespoons olive oil
- 1/2 cup freshly grated Parmesan cheese
- Salt and freshly ground black pepper, to taste
- Fresh parsley or basil, chopped (optional, for garnish)

Instructions:

1. Prepare the Broth:
   - In a saucepan, heat the chicken or vegetable broth over low heat. Keep it warm throughout the cooking process.
2. Sauté the Aromatics:
   - In a large, heavy-bottomed pot or Dutch oven, heat the olive oil and 1 tablespoon of butter over medium heat.
   - Add the finely chopped onion and sauté for 3-4 minutes until softened.
   - Add the minced garlic and cook for another 1-2 minutes until fragrant.
3. Toast the Rice:
   - Add the Arborio rice to the pot with the onions and garlic. Stir to coat the rice with the oil and cook for about 1-2 minutes until the rice grains are translucent around the edges.
4. Deglaze with Wine:
   - Pour in the dry white wine and stir constantly until it is absorbed by the rice.
5. Cook the Risotto:
   - Begin adding the warm broth to the rice mixture, one ladleful (about 1/2 cup) at a time.
   - Stir continuously and allow each addition of broth to be absorbed by the rice before adding the next ladleful. This process helps release the starch from the rice and creates a creamy texture.
   - Continue adding broth and stirring until the rice is creamy and cooked al dente, which should take about 18-20 minutes. You may not need all the broth, or you may need a little extra water if you run out of broth.
6. Finish the Risotto:
   - Once the rice is cooked to your desired texture (creamy with a slight bite), remove the pot from the heat.

- Stir in the remaining tablespoon of butter and grated Parmesan cheese until melted and well combined. Season with salt and freshly ground black pepper to taste.
7. Serve:
    - Spoon the risotto into serving bowls. Garnish with chopped fresh parsley or basil if desired.
    - Serve immediately while hot, as risotto has a tendency to continue absorbing liquid and can become dry upon standing.

Mario Batali's risotto recipe is a comforting and versatile dish that can be enjoyed as a main course or as a side dish with grilled meats or seafood. The key is patience in adding the broth gradually and stirring constantly to achieve the perfect creamy consistency. Enjoy the rich flavors and creamy texture of this classic Italian dish!

Paula Deen - Southern Fried Chicken

Ingredients:

- 1 whole chicken, cut into pieces (or use your preferred chicken parts like drumsticks, thighs, breasts, etc.)
- Salt and freshly ground black pepper
- 2 cups buttermilk
- 2 cups all-purpose flour
- 1 tablespoon paprika
- 1 tablespoon garlic powder
- 1 tablespoon onion powder
- 1 teaspoon cayenne pepper (optional, for heat)
- Vegetable oil, for frying

Instructions:

1. Prepare the Chicken:
    - Rinse the chicken pieces under cold water and pat dry with paper towels.
    - Season the chicken generously with salt and pepper.
2. Marinate in Buttermilk:
    - Place the seasoned chicken pieces in a large bowl or resealable plastic bag.
    - Pour the buttermilk over the chicken, making sure each piece is well coated.
    - Cover the bowl or seal the bag and refrigerate for at least 4 hours or overnight. This helps tenderize the chicken and adds flavor.
3. Prepare the Breading:
    - In a shallow dish or large bowl, combine the flour, paprika, garlic powder, onion powder, and cayenne pepper (if using).
    - Mix well to combine all the dry ingredients.
4. Coat the Chicken:
    - Remove the chicken pieces from the buttermilk, allowing any excess buttermilk to drip off.
    - Dredge each piece of chicken in the seasoned flour mixture, pressing gently to adhere the flour to the chicken.
5. Fry the Chicken:
    - In a large skillet or Dutch oven, heat about 1 inch of vegetable oil over medium-high heat until it reaches 350°F (175°C).
    - Carefully place the coated chicken pieces in the hot oil, skin side down if using skin-on pieces. Be careful not to overcrowd the pan; you may need to fry in batches.
    - Fry the chicken for about 6-8 minutes per side, or until golden brown and cooked through. The internal temperature should reach 165°F (75°C) for chicken to be fully cooked.
6. Drain and Serve:

- Remove the fried chicken from the oil and place on a wire rack or paper towels to drain excess oil.
- Serve hot, garnished with fresh herbs if desired.

Paula Deen's Southern Fried Chicken is best enjoyed fresh and crispy, served alongside your favorite sides like mashed potatoes, coleslaw, cornbread, or biscuits. It's a classic comfort food dish that brings the flavors of the South to your table.

Mary Berry - Victoria Sponge Cake

Ingredients:

For the cake:

- 1 cup (225g) unsalted butter, softened, plus extra for greasing
- 1 cup (225g) caster sugar (superfine sugar)
- 4 large eggs, at room temperature
- 2 cups (225g) self-raising flour
- 1 teaspoon baking powder
- 2 tablespoons milk

For the filling:

- Strawberry or raspberry jam (about 1/2 to 3/4 cup)
- 1/2 cup (120ml) heavy cream, whipped
- Powdered sugar, for dusting (optional)

Instructions:

1. Preheat and Prepare:
    - Preheat your oven to 350°F (180°C). Grease and line two 8-inch (20cm) round cake tins with parchment paper.
2. Make the Cake:
    - In a large mixing bowl, cream together the softened butter and caster sugar until pale and fluffy.
    - Add the eggs, one at a time, beating well after each addition.
    - Sift the self-raising flour and baking powder into the bowl. Gently fold the flour into the mixture until well combined.
    - Add the milk and fold gently until you have a smooth batter.
3. Bake the Cakes:
    - Divide the batter evenly between the prepared cake tins and smooth the tops with a spatula.
    - Bake in the preheated oven for 20-25 minutes, or until the cakes are golden and spring back when lightly touched.
    - Remove from the oven and let the cakes cool in the tins for 5 minutes. Then, turn them out onto a wire rack to cool completely.
4. Assemble the Cake:
    - Once the cakes are completely cool, place one cake layer on a serving plate or cake stand.
    - Spread a generous layer of strawberry or raspberry jam over the top of the cake layer.
    - In a separate bowl, whip the heavy cream until it forms soft peaks. Spread the whipped cream over the jam layer.

5. Finish:
    - Place the second cake layer on top of the whipped cream layer.
    - Dust the top of the cake with powdered sugar if desired.
6. Serve:
    - Slice and serve the Victoria Sponge Cake as a delightful dessert or afternoon treat.

Mary Berry's Victoria Sponge Cake is a timeless classic that showcases the simplicity and elegance of British baking. It's perfect for sharing with friends and family, paired with a cup of tea or coffee. Enjoy the light, fluffy texture and delicious flavors of this beloved cake!

David Chang - Ramen

Ingredients:

For the broth:

- 8 cups (2 liters) chicken broth (homemade or store-bought)
- 2 cups (480ml) water
- 2-3 garlic cloves, minced
- 1-inch piece of ginger, peeled and minced
- 2 tablespoons soy sauce
- 2 tablespoons mirin (Japanese sweet rice wine)
- 1 tablespoon sesame oil
- Salt, to taste

For the ramen:

- 4 servings of ramen noodles (fresh or dried)
- 4 soft-boiled eggs, halved (optional)
- 2 cups shredded cooked chicken or pork belly (optional)
- Sliced green onions (scallions), for garnish
- Nori (seaweed sheets), torn into pieces (optional)
- Sesame seeds, for garnish (optional)

Instructions:

1. Prepare the Broth:
   - In a large pot, combine the chicken broth, water, minced garlic, minced ginger, soy sauce, mirin, and sesame oil.
   - Bring to a boil over medium-high heat, then reduce the heat and let it simmer for at least 30 minutes to allow the flavors to meld. Season with salt to taste.
2. Prepare the Ramen Noodles:
   - Cook the ramen noodles according to the package instructions until al dente. Drain and set aside.
3. Assemble the Ramen Bowls:
   - Divide the cooked ramen noodles among serving bowls.
   - Ladle the hot broth over the noodles, making sure each bowl gets a generous amount of broth.
4. Add Toppings:
   - Arrange the soft-boiled eggs (halved), shredded cooked chicken or pork belly (if using), sliced green onions, torn nori sheets, and sesame seeds on top of each bowl.
5. Serve:
   - Serve the ramen hot, allowing diners to mix the toppings into the broth as they eat.

David Chang's style of ramen often emphasizes bold flavors, balanced with rich broth and a variety of toppings. Feel free to customize your ramen with additional ingredients such as bamboo shoots, corn kernels, bean sprouts, or marinated mushrooms. This homemade ramen captures the essence of Chang's approach to comforting, flavorful food that satisfies both the palate and the soul. Enjoy your delicious bowl of ramen!

Bobby Flay - Fish Tacos

Ingredients:

For the fish:

- 1 pound (450g) white fish fillets (such as cod, tilapia, or mahi-mahi), cut into strips
- 1 tablespoon olive oil
- 1 tablespoon chili powder
- 1 teaspoon ground cumin
- 1 teaspoon smoked paprika
- Salt and freshly ground black pepper, to taste
- Juice of 1 lime

For the slaw:

- 2 cups shredded cabbage (green or purple cabbage or a mix)
- 1/4 cup chopped fresh cilantro
- 1 jalapeño, seeded and finely chopped (optional for heat)
- 1 tablespoon olive oil
- Juice of 1 lime
- Salt and freshly ground black pepper, to taste

For serving:

- 8 small flour or corn tortillas, warmed
- Avocado slices, for garnish
- Fresh cilantro leaves, for garnish
- Lime wedges, for serving
- Hot sauce or salsa, optional

Instructions:

1. Prepare the Fish:
   - In a bowl, combine the olive oil, chili powder, cumin, smoked paprika, salt, pepper, and lime juice to make a marinade.
   - Add the fish strips to the marinade, tossing gently to coat evenly. Let it marinate for about 15-20 minutes while you prepare the slaw and other ingredients.
2. Make the Slaw:
   - In another bowl, combine the shredded cabbage, chopped cilantro, chopped jalapeño (if using), olive oil, lime juice, salt, and pepper. Toss well to combine. Set aside.
3. Cook the Fish:
   - Heat a grill pan or skillet over medium-high heat. Brush with a little oil to prevent sticking.

- Cook the marinated fish strips for 2-3 minutes per side, or until cooked through and lightly charred. Alternatively, you can bake the fish in a preheated oven at 400°F (200°C) for about 10-12 minutes, flipping halfway through.
4. Assemble the Tacos:
    - Warm the tortillas on the grill or in a dry skillet for about 30 seconds per side until soft and pliable.
    - Place a few pieces of cooked fish on each tortilla.
    - Top with a generous spoonful of the prepared slaw.
    - Garnish with avocado slices, fresh cilantro leaves, and a squeeze of lime juice.
5. Serve:
    - Serve the fish tacos immediately, with lime wedges and optional hot sauce or salsa on the side.

Bobby Flay's fish tacos are bursting with fresh flavors and textures, combining the smoky spice of the fish with the crispness of the slaw and the creaminess of avocado. They make for a delicious and satisfying meal, perfect for any occasion! Enjoy these vibrant and flavorful tacos inspired by Bobby Flay's culinary style.

Rachel Khoo - Croissants

Ingredients:

For the dough:

- 2 cups (250g) all-purpose flour, plus extra for dusting
- 1/4 cup (50g) granulated sugar
- 1 teaspoon salt
- 2 1/4 teaspoons (7g or 1 packet) active dry yeast
- 1/2 cup (120ml) warm water (about 110°F or 45°C)
- 1/2 cup (120ml) cold milk
- 1 cup (225g) unsalted butter, cold

For the butter block:

- 1 cup (225g) unsalted butter, cold
- 1 tablespoon all-purpose flour, for dusting

For finishing:

- 1 egg, beaten (for egg wash)
- Powdered sugar, for dusting (optional)

Instructions:

1. Prepare the Dough:
   - In a large mixing bowl, combine the flour, sugar, and salt.
   - In a separate bowl, dissolve the yeast in warm water and let it sit for 5-10 minutes until frothy.
   - Add the yeast mixture and cold milk to the flour mixture. Stir until a rough dough forms.
2. Knead the Dough:
   - Turn the dough out onto a lightly floured surface and knead for about 5-7 minutes until smooth and elastic.
   - Shape the dough into a ball, cover with plastic wrap, and refrigerate for 30 minutes to relax the gluten.
3. Prepare the Butter Block:
   - While the dough is resting, prepare the butter block. On a piece of parchment paper, sprinkle the tablespoon of flour.
   - Place the cold butter on top of the flour and sprinkle another tablespoon of flour over the butter.
   - Fold the parchment paper over the butter and pound it with a rolling pin until it forms a flat, 6x8-inch (15x20cm) rectangle. Chill in the refrigerator for 10-15 minutes if it becomes too soft.

4. Laminate the Dough:
   - On a lightly floured surface, roll out the chilled dough into a 10x16-inch (25x40cm) rectangle.
   - Place the chilled butter block in the center of the dough rectangle, with the short side of the butter block parallel to the long side of the dough rectangle.
   - Fold one-third of the dough over the butter block, then fold the other third over the top, like folding a letter.
5. First Turn:
   - Rotate the dough 90 degrees so that the open ends are at the top and bottom (like a book).
   - Roll out the dough again into a 10x16-inch (25x40cm) rectangle.
   - Fold the dough in thirds again, wrap in plastic wrap, and refrigerate for 30 minutes.
6. Second Turn:
   - Remove the dough from the refrigerator, unwrap, and place it on a lightly floured surface.
   - Again, roll out the dough into a 10x16-inch (25x40cm) rectangle and fold it in thirds.
   - Wrap in plastic wrap and refrigerate for another 30 minutes.
7. Third Turn:
   - Repeat the rolling and folding process one more time (roll out into a 10x16-inch rectangle and fold in thirds).
   - Wrap the dough tightly in plastic wrap and refrigerate overnight, or for at least 4-6 hours.
8. Shape and Bake the Croissants:
   - On a lightly floured surface, roll out the chilled dough into a large rectangle, about 1/4-inch thick.
   - Cut the dough into triangles (about 4-5 inches wide at the base).
   - Starting from the base of each triangle, roll the dough up towards the tip to form a crescent shape.
   - Place the shaped croissants on a baking sheet lined with parchment paper, leaving space between each one.
   - Cover loosely with plastic wrap and let them rise at room temperature for 1-2 hours, until they have doubled in size.
9. Bake the Croissants:
   - Preheat your oven to 400°F (200°C).
   - Brush the risen croissants with beaten egg wash.
   - Bake in the preheated oven for 15-20 minutes, or until golden brown and flaky.
10. Finish:
    - Remove from the oven and let cool on a wire rack.
    - Optionally, dust with powdered sugar before serving.

Rachel Khoo's croissants are a labor of love but well worth the effort for their buttery, flaky texture and delicious flavor. Enjoy these homemade croissants warm from the oven for a delightful breakfast or snack!

Marcus Samuelsson - Jerk Chicken

Ingredients:

For the marinade:

- 2-3 pounds (about 1-1.5 kg) chicken pieces (drumsticks, thighs, breasts)
- 1/4 cup soy sauce
- Juice of 2 limes
- 1/4 cup olive oil
- 4 cloves garlic, minced
- 1 tablespoon fresh ginger, grated
- 2 tablespoons brown sugar
- 2 tablespoons fresh thyme leaves (or 2 teaspoons dried thyme)
- 2 teaspoons ground allspice
- 1 teaspoon ground cinnamon
- 1 teaspoon ground nutmeg
- 1 teaspoon cayenne pepper (adjust to taste for spiciness)
- Salt and freshly ground black pepper, to taste

For serving:

- Cooked rice or Jamaican rice and peas
- Sliced fresh pineapple or mango (optional)
- Lime wedges
- Fresh cilantro or parsley, chopped

Instructions:

1. Prepare the Marinade:
    - In a bowl, combine the soy sauce, lime juice, olive oil, minced garlic, grated ginger, brown sugar, thyme, allspice, cinnamon, nutmeg, cayenne pepper, salt, and black pepper. Mix well to combine.
2. Marinate the Chicken:
    - Place the chicken pieces in a large resealable plastic bag or a shallow dish.
    - Pour the marinade over the chicken, making sure each piece is well coated.
    - Seal the bag or cover the dish with plastic wrap and refrigerate for at least 2-4 hours, or preferably overnight, to allow the flavors to meld and the chicken to absorb the marinade.
3. Grill or Bake the Chicken:
    - Preheat your grill to medium-high heat (around 375-400°F or 190-200°C). You can also bake the chicken in a preheated oven at 400°F (200°C) if preferred.
    - If grilling, lightly oil the grill grates. Remove the chicken from the marinade, shaking off any excess, and place it on the grill.

- Grill the chicken for about 6-8 minutes per side, or until it reaches an internal temperature of 165°F (75°C) and is cooked through. Turn occasionally and baste with any remaining marinade.
4. Rest and Serve:
    - Once cooked through, remove the jerk chicken from the grill and let it rest for a few minutes before serving.
    - Serve the jerk chicken hot with cooked rice or Jamaican rice and peas.
    - Garnish with sliced fresh pineapple or mango (if using), lime wedges, and chopped fresh cilantro or parsley.

Marcus Samuelsson's Jerk Chicken is flavorful, aromatic, and spicy with a hint of sweetness from the marinade. It captures the essence of Caribbean cuisine and is perfect for a summer barbecue or any occasion where you want to impress with bold flavors. Enjoy this delicious dish with family and friends!

Yotam Ottolenghi - Mediterranean Salad

Ingredients:

For the salad:

- 1 cup cherry tomatoes, halved
- 1 cucumber, diced
- 1 red bell pepper, diced
- 1/2 red onion, thinly sliced
- 1/2 cup Kalamata olives, pitted
- 1/2 cup feta cheese, crumbled
- 1/4 cup fresh parsley, chopped
- 1/4 cup fresh mint leaves, chopped

For the dressing:

- 1/4 cup extra-virgin olive oil
- Juice of 1 lemon
- 1 garlic clove, minced
- 1 teaspoon dried oregano
- Salt and freshly ground black pepper, to taste

Instructions:

1. Prepare the Salad:
    - In a large salad bowl, combine the cherry tomatoes, diced cucumber, diced red bell pepper, thinly sliced red onion, Kalamata olives, crumbled feta cheese, chopped parsley, and chopped mint leaves.
2. Make the Dressing:
    - In a small bowl or jar, whisk together the extra-virgin olive oil, lemon juice, minced garlic, dried oregano, salt, and black pepper until well combined.
3. Assemble the Salad:
    - Drizzle the dressing over the salad ingredients in the bowl.
    - Gently toss the salad until everything is evenly coated with the dressing.
4. Serve:
    - Transfer the Mediterranean salad to a serving platter or individual salad plates.
    - Optionally, garnish with additional fresh herbs or a sprinkle of feta cheese.
    - Serve immediately and enjoy as a refreshing and flavorful side dish or light lunch.

Yotam Ottolenghi's Mediterranean Salad celebrates the bright colors and robust flavors of the Mediterranean region. It's a perfect balance of fresh vegetables, tangy olives, creamy feta cheese, and aromatic herbs, all brought together with a zesty lemon and garlic dressing. This salad is not only delicious but also showcases Ottolenghi's philosophy of letting quality ingredients shine.

Thomas Keller - Beef Short Ribs

Ingredients:

- 4 beef short ribs, bone-in (about 2-3 pounds total)
- Salt and freshly ground black pepper
- 2 tablespoons vegetable oil
- 1 onion, chopped
- 2 carrots, chopped
- 2 celery stalks, chopped
- 4 garlic cloves, minced
- 2 cups red wine (such as Cabernet Sauvignon)
- 2 cups beef broth
- 2-3 sprigs fresh thyme
- 2-3 sprigs fresh rosemary
- 1 bay leaf
- Mashed potatoes or creamy polenta, for serving
- Chopped fresh parsley, for garnish (optional)

Instructions:

1. Preheat and Prepare:
    - Preheat your oven to 325°F (160°C).
2. Season and Sear the Short Ribs:
    - Pat the beef short ribs dry with paper towels and season generously with salt and pepper.
    - Heat the vegetable oil in a large oven-safe Dutch oven or heavy-bottomed pot over medium-high heat.
    - Add the short ribs to the pot, in batches if necessary to avoid overcrowding, and sear on all sides until well browned. This step helps develop flavor and a nice crust on the meat. Remove the ribs and set aside.
3. Cook the Vegetables:
    - In the same pot, add the chopped onion, carrots, and celery. Cook, stirring occasionally, until the vegetables are softened and lightly browned, about 5-7 minutes.
    - Add the minced garlic and cook for another 1-2 minutes until fragrant.
4. Deglaze and Add Liquid:
    - Pour in the red wine and bring to a simmer, scraping up any browned bits from the bottom of the pot.
    - Add the beef broth, fresh thyme, rosemary sprigs, and bay leaf. Stir to combine.
5. Braise the Short Ribs:
    - Return the seared short ribs to the pot, nestling them into the liquid and vegetables.
    - Bring the liquid to a simmer again, then cover the pot with a lid or foil.

6. Bake in the Oven:
    - Transfer the covered pot to the preheated oven and braise the short ribs for about 2.5 to 3 hours, or until the meat is fork-tender and falling off the bone.
7. Serve:
    - Remove the pot from the oven and carefully transfer the short ribs to a serving platter.
    - Strain the braising liquid through a fine-mesh sieve, discarding the solids, to create a smooth sauce.
    - Serve the beef short ribs over mashed potatoes or creamy polenta, spooning some of the sauce over the top.
    - Garnish with chopped fresh parsley if desired.

Thomas Keller's beef short ribs are rich, tender, and infused with the flavors of red wine and aromatic herbs. This dish is perfect for a special occasion or when you want to impress with a comforting and hearty meal. Enjoy the melt-in-your-mouth goodness of these braised beef short ribs!

Carla Hall - Biscuits and Gravy

Ingredients:

For the biscuits:

- 2 cups all-purpose flour, plus extra for dusting
- 1 tablespoon baking powder
- 1/2 teaspoon baking soda
- 1 teaspoon salt
- 6 tablespoons unsalted butter, cold and cut into cubes
- 3/4 cup buttermilk

For the sausage gravy:

- 1/2 pound breakfast sausage (pork or turkey)
- 2 tablespoons unsalted butter
- 1/4 cup all-purpose flour
- 3 cups whole milk
- Salt and freshly ground black pepper, to taste
- Pinch of cayenne pepper (optional, for a hint of heat)

Instructions:

1. Make the Biscuits:
    - Preheat your oven to 450°F (230°C).
    - In a large mixing bowl, whisk together the flour, baking powder, baking soda, and salt.
    - Add the cold butter cubes to the flour mixture. Using your fingertips or a pastry cutter, quickly work the butter into the flour until the mixture resembles coarse crumbs with some larger pea-sized pieces of butter remaining.
    - Make a well in the center of the flour mixture and pour in the buttermilk. Stir gently with a wooden spoon or rubber spatula until just combined and the dough comes together.
2. Shape and Bake the Biscuits:
    - Turn the dough out onto a lightly floured surface. Pat or roll the dough to a thickness of about 1 inch.
    - Using a floured biscuit cutter or a drinking glass, cut out rounds of dough and place them on a baking sheet lined with parchment paper, making sure they are touching each other slightly.
    - Gather any scraps of dough, gently pat together, and cut out more biscuits.
    - Bake the biscuits in the preheated oven for 10-12 minutes, or until golden brown on top. Remove from the oven and set aside.
3. Make the Sausage Gravy:

- While the biscuits are baking, cook the breakfast sausage in a large skillet over medium-high heat, breaking it up into crumbles with a spatula or wooden spoon. Cook until browned and cooked through, about 5-7 minutes.
- Remove the cooked sausage from the skillet with a slotted spoon and set aside, leaving the drippings in the skillet.
- Reduce the heat to medium-low and add the butter to the skillet. Once melted, sprinkle the flour evenly over the butter and sausage drippings. Cook, stirring constantly, for 1-2 minutes to make a roux.

4. Finish the Gravy:
    - Gradually pour in the milk, whisking constantly to prevent lumps from forming.
    - Cook the gravy, stirring frequently, until it thickens and reaches your desired consistency, about 5-7 minutes.
    - Stir in the cooked sausage and season the gravy with salt, pepper, and a pinch of cayenne pepper if using.
5. Serve:
    - Split the warm biscuits in half and place them on serving plates.
    - Spoon generous amounts of sausage gravy over the biscuits.
    - Serve immediately, garnished with freshly ground black pepper if desired.

Carla Hall's biscuits and gravy are a comforting and satisfying dish, perfect for breakfast or brunch. The fluffy biscuits pair perfectly with the creamy, flavorful sausage gravy, making it a Southern classic that will warm your heart and fill your belly. Enjoy this delicious taste of Southern hospitality!

Alex Guarnaschelli - Beef Stroganoff

Ingredients:

- 1 pound (450g) beef sirloin or tenderloin, thinly sliced into strips
- Salt and freshly ground black pepper, to taste
- 2 tablespoons olive oil
- 1 onion, finely chopped
- 2 cloves garlic, minced
- 8 ounces (225g) cremini mushrooms, sliced
- 1 tablespoon all-purpose flour
- 1 cup beef broth
- 1 tablespoon Dijon mustard
- 1 tablespoon Worcestershire sauce
- 1/2 cup sour cream
- 1/4 cup heavy cream or half-and-half
- Chopped fresh parsley, for garnish
- Cooked egg noodles or rice, for serving

Instructions:

1. Prepare the Beef:
   - Season the beef strips with salt and pepper.
   - In a large skillet or sauté pan, heat 1 tablespoon of olive oil over medium-high heat.
   - Add the beef strips in batches and cook until browned on all sides, about 1-2 minutes per side. Remove the beef from the skillet and set aside.
2. Cook the Vegetables:
   - In the same skillet, add the remaining 1 tablespoon of olive oil.
   - Add the chopped onion and cook until softened and translucent, about 3-4 minutes.
   - Add the minced garlic and sliced mushrooms. Cook, stirring occasionally, until the mushrooms are tender and any liquid has evaporated, about 5-7 minutes.
3. Make the Sauce:
   - Sprinkle the flour over the cooked vegetables in the skillet. Stir constantly for 1-2 minutes to cook the flour.
   - Gradually add the beef broth, stirring constantly to prevent lumps.
   - Stir in the Dijon mustard and Worcestershire sauce. Bring the mixture to a simmer and cook for 3-4 minutes, or until slightly thickened.
4. Finish the Stroganoff:
   - Reduce the heat to low. Stir in the sour cream and heavy cream or half-and-half until well combined.
   - Return the cooked beef strips to the skillet and simmer gently for another 2-3 minutes to heat through and allow flavors to meld.

            - Season with additional salt and pepper to taste.
    5. Serve:
        - Serve the Beef Stroganoff hot over cooked egg noodles or rice.
        - Garnish with chopped fresh parsley before serving.

Alex Guarnaschelli's Beef Stroganoff is creamy, comforting, and packed with savory flavors from the mushrooms, beef, and rich sauce. It's a satisfying dish that's perfect for a cozy dinner at home. Enjoy this delicious take on a classic comfort food!

Jose Andres - Paella

Ingredients:

- 1 cup Spanish paella rice (such as Bomba or Calasparra)
- 4 cups chicken broth (or seafood broth for a seafood paella)
- 1/4 cup olive oil
- 1 onion, finely chopped
- 4 cloves garlic, minced
- 1 red bell pepper, thinly sliced
- 1 tomato, grated or finely chopped
- 1 pinch saffron threads (about 1/2 teaspoon)
- 1 teaspoon smoked paprika
- Salt and freshly ground black pepper, to taste
- 1 pound (450g) mixed seafood (such as shrimp, squid, mussels, and/or clams)
- 1/2 cup frozen peas (optional)
- Lemon wedges, for serving

Instructions:

1. Prepare the Ingredients:
    - If using seafood like shrimp or squid, clean and prepare them as needed. Scrub mussels and clams under cold water and discard any that do not close when tapped.
2. Prepare the Broth:
    - In a saucepan, heat the chicken broth until hot. Add the saffron threads to infuse the broth with flavor. Keep the broth warm over low heat.
3. Cook the Base:
    - In a large paella pan or wide skillet, heat the olive oil over medium heat.
    - Add the chopped onion and cook until softened, about 3-4 minutes.
    - Add the minced garlic and sliced red bell pepper. Cook for another 2-3 minutes until the vegetables are tender.
4. Add Rice and Seasonings:
    - Stir in the grated or finely chopped tomato and cook for 2-3 minutes until it starts to break down.
    - Sprinkle the smoked paprika over the vegetables and stir to combine.
    - Add the paella rice to the pan, stirring to coat the rice with the oil and vegetables. Cook for 1-2 minutes to toast the rice slightly.
5. Cook the Paella:
    - Pour the hot saffron-infused broth into the pan, stirring gently to distribute the ingredients evenly.
    - Season with salt and pepper to taste. Bring the mixture to a simmer.
6. Add the Seafood and Peas:

- Arrange the mixed seafood (shrimp, squid, mussels, clams) evenly over the rice mixture.
- If using frozen peas, sprinkle them over the top.
7. Simmer and Finish:
    - Reduce the heat to medium-low and let the paella simmer, without stirring, for about 20-25 minutes. Rotate the pan occasionally to ensure even cooking.
    - The paella is done when the rice is tender and has absorbed the liquid, and the seafood is cooked through (shrimp should be pink, mussels and clams should open).
8. Serve:
    - Remove the paella from the heat and let it rest for 5 minutes.
    - Garnish with lemon wedges and serve hot directly from the pan.

Jose Andres' paella is a celebration of Spanish flavors, with tender rice infused with saffron and a delightful assortment of seafood. It's a dish that brings people together and captures the essence of Spanish culinary tradition. Enjoy this delicious and communal meal with friends and family!

Ainsley Harriott - Jamaican Jerk Chicken

Ingredients:

For the Jerk Marinade:

- 4-6 chicken leg quarters or chicken pieces (about 2-3 lbs)
- 3-4 green onions (scallions), chopped
- 4 garlic cloves, chopped
- 1-2 Scotch bonnet peppers, seeds removed (adjust to taste for spiciness)
- 1 tablespoon fresh thyme leaves (or 1 teaspoon dried thyme)
- 1 tablespoon ground allspice
- 1 tablespoon brown sugar
- 1 tablespoon soy sauce
- 1 tablespoon vegetable oil
- Juice of 1 lime
- Salt and freshly ground black pepper, to taste

For serving:

- Cooked rice and peas (traditional Jamaican rice and kidney beans dish)
- Sliced fresh mango or pineapple (optional, for garnish)
- Lime wedges

Instructions:

1. Prepare the Jerk Marinade:
   - In a food processor or blender, combine the chopped green onions, garlic cloves, Scotch bonnet peppers, thyme leaves, ground allspice, brown sugar, soy sauce, vegetable oil, lime juice, salt, and pepper.
   - Blend until smooth to create the jerk marinade. Adjust seasoning and spiciness level to your taste.
2. Marinate the Chicken:
   - Place the chicken pieces in a large resealable plastic bag or a shallow dish.
   - Pour the jerk marinade over the chicken, ensuring each piece is well coated. Massage the marinade into the chicken.
   - Seal the bag or cover the dish with plastic wrap and refrigerate for at least 4 hours, or preferably overnight, to allow the flavors to penetrate the chicken.
3. Grill or Bake the Jerk Chicken:
   - Preheat your grill to medium-high heat (around 375-400°F or 190-200°C). You can also bake the chicken in a preheated oven at 400°F (200°C) if preferred.
   - If grilling, lightly oil the grill grates. Remove the chicken from the marinade, shaking off any excess marinade.

- Grill the chicken for about 6-8 minutes per side, or until it reaches an internal temperature of 165°F (75°C) and is cooked through. Turn occasionally and baste with any remaining marinade.
4. Rest and Serve:
    - Once cooked through, remove the jerk chicken from the grill and let it rest for a few minutes before serving.
    - Serve the Jamaican Jerk Chicken hot with cooked rice and peas (rice and kidney beans dish).
    - Garnish with sliced fresh mango or pineapple (if using) and lime wedges on the side.

Ainsley Harriott's Jamaican Jerk Chicken is spicy, aromatic, and full of Caribbean flavors. It's a dish that's perfect for a festive gathering or a taste of island cuisine at home. Enjoy the vibrant and bold flavors of this delicious Jamaican classic!

Rick Bayless - Guacamole

Ingredients:

- 3 ripe avocados
- 1/4 cup finely chopped onion (preferably red onion)
- 1-2 serrano or jalapeño peppers, seeded and minced (adjust to taste for spiciness)
- 1/4 cup chopped fresh cilantro
- Juice of 1 lime
- 1/2 teaspoon salt, or more to taste
- 1/4 teaspoon freshly ground black pepper
- Optional: 1 small tomato, seeded and diced

Instructions:

1. Prepare the Avocados:
    - Cut each avocado in half lengthwise. Remove the pit and scoop the avocado flesh into a mixing bowl.
2. Mash the Avocados:
    - Using a fork or potato masher, mash the avocado until it reaches your desired consistency (smooth or slightly chunky).
3. Add the Remaining Ingredients:
    - Add the finely chopped onion, minced serrano or jalapeño peppers, chopped cilantro, lime juice, salt, and black pepper to the mashed avocado.
4. Mix Well:
    - Gently stir all the ingredients together until well combined. Taste and adjust seasoning as needed, adding more salt, lime juice, or peppers if desired.
5. Optional: Add Diced Tomato:
    - If using tomato, gently fold in the diced tomato at this stage.
6. Serve:
    - Transfer the guacamole to a serving bowl.
    - Serve immediately with tortilla chips, tacos, quesadillas, or alongside your favorite Mexican dishes.

Rick Bayless' guacamole is fresh, vibrant, and bursting with flavor from the creamy avocados, zesty lime juice, and aromatic cilantro. It's a perfect appetizer or side dish that highlights the simplicity and deliciousness of authentic Mexican cuisine. Enjoy this homemade guacamole with family and friends!

Gino D'Acampo - Tiramisu

Ingredients:

- 250g mascarpone cheese
- 300ml double cream (heavy cream)
- 3 tablespoons caster sugar
- 1 teaspoon vanilla extract
- 200ml strong espresso coffee, cooled
- 2 tablespoons coffee liqueur (optional)
- 24-30 ladyfinger biscuits (savoiardi)
- Cocoa powder, for dusting
- Dark chocolate shavings, for garnish (optional)

Instructions:

1. Prepare the Espresso:
    - Brew strong espresso coffee and allow it to cool to room temperature. You can add coffee liqueur to the coffee if desired, for extra flavor.
2. Prepare the Mascarpone Mixture:
    - In a large mixing bowl, combine the mascarpone cheese, double cream, caster sugar, and vanilla extract.
    - Using an electric mixer or whisk, beat the mixture until it becomes thick and creamy. Be careful not to overmix.
3. Assemble the Tiramisu:
    - Dip each ladyfinger biscuit into the cooled espresso coffee mixture briefly (don't soak them completely) and arrange them in a single layer in the bottom of a serving dish or individual glasses.
    - Spread half of the mascarpone mixture evenly over the layer of soaked ladyfingers.
4. Repeat the Layers:
    - Repeat with another layer of dipped ladyfingers and the remaining mascarpone mixture on top.
5. Chill and Serve:
    - Cover the dish or glasses with plastic wrap and refrigerate for at least 4 hours, or ideally overnight, to allow the flavors to meld and the tiramisu to set.
6. Finish and Garnish:
    - Before serving, dust the top of the tiramisu with cocoa powder using a fine sieve.
    - Optionally, garnish with dark chocolate shavings for added texture and flavor.

Gino D'Acampo's Tiramisu is creamy, indulgent, and perfect for any occasion, whether you're entertaining guests or enjoying a special dessert at home. It captures the essence of Italian cuisine with its delicate balance of coffee-soaked biscuits and creamy mascarpone filling. Buon appetito!

Anne Burrell - Spaghetti and Meatballs

Ingredients:

For the meatballs:

- 1 pound (450g) ground beef (or a mix of beef and pork)
- 1/2 cup breadcrumbs
- 1/4 cup grated Parmesan cheese
- 1/4 cup chopped fresh parsley
- 1 egg
- 2 cloves garlic, minced
- 1 teaspoon salt
- 1/2 teaspoon black pepper
- Olive oil, for frying

For the tomato sauce:

- 2 tablespoons olive oil
- 1 onion, finely chopped
- 2 cloves garlic, minced
- 1 (28-ounce) can crushed tomatoes
- 1 (14-ounce) can diced tomatoes
- 1 teaspoon dried oregano
- 1 teaspoon dried basil
- Salt and pepper, to taste

For serving:

- 1 pound (450g) spaghetti
- Grated Parmesan cheese, for garnish
- Chopped fresh basil or parsley, for garnish

Instructions:

1. Make the Meatballs:
    - In a large mixing bowl, combine the ground beef, breadcrumbs, grated Parmesan cheese, chopped parsley, egg, minced garlic, salt, and pepper.
    - Mix together gently using your hands until well combined.
    - Shape the mixture into meatballs, about 1-2 inches in diameter.
2. Cook the Meatballs:
    - Heat a couple of tablespoons of olive oil in a large skillet over medium-high heat.
    - Add the meatballs in batches, making sure not to overcrowd the pan. Cook until browned on all sides, about 6-8 minutes. Remove the meatballs and set aside.
3. Make the Tomato Sauce:

- In the same skillet, add 2 tablespoons of olive oil if needed.
- Add the finely chopped onion and cook until softened, about 5 minutes.
- Add the minced garlic and cook for another minute until fragrant.
- Stir in the crushed tomatoes, diced tomatoes (with their juices), dried oregano, and dried basil. Season with salt and pepper to taste.
- Bring the sauce to a simmer and cook for about 15-20 minutes, stirring occasionally, until the flavors meld together and the sauce thickens slightly.

4. Cook the Spaghetti:
    - Meanwhile, bring a large pot of salted water to a boil.
    - Cook the spaghetti according to the package instructions until al dente. Drain well.
5. Combine and Serve:
    - Add the cooked meatballs to the simmering tomato sauce and let them heat through for a few minutes.
    - Serve the spaghetti topped with the meatballs and sauce.
    - Garnish with grated Parmesan cheese and chopped fresh basil or parsley.

Anne Burrell's Spaghetti and Meatballs is a comforting and satisfying meal that brings together tender meatballs, flavorful tomato sauce, and perfectly cooked spaghetti. It's a timeless favorite that's sure to please family and friends alike. Enjoy this delicious taste of Italian-American cuisine!

Curtis Stone - Grilled Steak

Ingredients:

- 2 (8-ounce) beef steaks (such as ribeye, sirloin, or New York strip), about 1-inch thick
- Salt and freshly ground black pepper
- 2 tablespoons olive oil
- Optional: Garlic cloves or herbs for additional flavor

Instructions:

1. Prepare the Steak:
    - Remove the steaks from the refrigerator about 30 minutes before cooking to allow them to come to room temperature. This helps ensure even cooking.
2. Preheat the Grill:
    - Preheat your grill to medium-high heat. Make sure the grill grates are clean and lightly oiled to prevent sticking.
3. Season the Steak:
    - Pat the steaks dry with paper towels. Season both sides generously with salt and freshly ground black pepper.
    - Drizzle olive oil over both sides of the steaks and rub it in gently. This helps to create a flavorful crust during grilling.
4. Grill the Steak:
    - Place the steaks on the preheated grill. For medium-rare, grill for about 4-5 minutes per side, or until an instant-read thermometer inserted into the thickest part of the steak registers 130-135°F (54-57°C).
    - Adjust cooking time according to your desired level of doneness: 3-4 minutes per side for rare, 5-6 minutes per side for medium, or 7-8 minutes per side for well-done.
    - Optional: For added flavor, you can add garlic cloves or fresh herbs (such as rosemary or thyme) to the grill during the last few minutes of cooking, or brush the steaks with herb butter after grilling.
5. Rest and Serve:
    - Once cooked to your liking, transfer the steaks to a cutting board or plate and let them rest for 5-10 minutes. This allows the juices to redistribute evenly throughout the meat.
6. Slice and Enjoy:
    - After resting, slice the steaks against the grain into thin strips.
    - Serve immediately, garnished with additional salt and pepper if desired.

Curtis Stone's grilled steak method ensures tender, juicy steaks with a delicious charred exterior. It's a simple yet impressive dish that highlights the natural flavors of the meat. Enjoy your grilled steak alongside your favorite sides, such as roasted vegetables, salad, or crispy potatoes.

Nancy Silverton - Artisan Bread

Ingredients:

- 3 cups (360g) bread flour (plus extra for dusting)
- 1 1/4 teaspoons salt
- 1/4 teaspoon instant yeast
- 1 1/2 cups (350ml) lukewarm water

Instructions:

1. Mixing the Dough:
   - In a large mixing bowl, combine the bread flour, salt, and instant yeast.
   - Gradually add the lukewarm water, stirring with a wooden spoon or your hands, until a shaggy dough forms and all the flour is incorporated. The dough will be sticky and rough.
2. First Rise (Bulk Fermentation):
   - Cover the bowl with plastic wrap or a clean kitchen towel.
   - Let the dough rest at room temperature for 12-18 hours (overnight is ideal), allowing it to ferment and develop flavor. The dough should roughly double in size and develop bubbles on the surface.
3. Shaping the Dough:
   - Generously flour a work surface. Scrape the dough out of the bowl onto the floured surface.
   - Gently fold the edges of the dough towards the center, creating a round shape.
   - Optionally, you can sprinkle a bit of flour over the top of the dough to prevent sticking.
4. Second Rise (Proofing):
   - Place the shaped dough onto a piece of parchment paper and cover it loosely with a kitchen towel.
   - Let the dough rise for another 1-2 hours at room temperature, until it increases in size by about 50% and springs back slowly when gently pressed with a finger.
5. Preheat the Oven:
   - About 30 minutes before baking, preheat your oven to 450°F (230°C). Place a Dutch oven or a heavy, oven-safe pot with a lid inside the oven as it preheats.
6. Baking the Bread:
   - Once the oven is preheated, carefully remove the hot pot from the oven.
   - Lift the risen dough using the parchment paper and place it into the hot pot. Be careful as the pot will be very hot.
   - Cover the pot with the lid and bake for 30 minutes.
7. Finishing the Bread:
   - After 30 minutes, remove the lid from the pot and continue baking for another 10-15 minutes, or until the bread is deep golden brown and sounds hollow when tapped on the bottom.

8. Cooling:
    - Transfer the bread to a wire rack and let it cool completely before slicing. This allows the crumb to set and develop.

Nancy Silverton's artisan bread is characterized by a crisp crust and an airy, chewy crumb with a complex flavor profile developed through slow fermentation. This simple method produces bread with a rustic appearance and a depth of flavor that makes it perfect for serving with soups, salads, or as a standalone treat with butter or olive oil. Enjoy the process of baking and the delicious results!

Lidia Bastianich - Gnocchi

Ingredients:

- 2 pounds (about 900g) russet potatoes (about 3 large potatoes)
- 1 1/2 cups (180g) all-purpose flour, plus extra for dusting
- 1 egg, lightly beaten
- Salt, to taste

Instructions:

1. Cook the Potatoes:
    - Place the whole potatoes (with skin on) in a large pot of salted water.
    - Bring to a boil over medium-high heat and cook until the potatoes are fork-tender, about 30-40 minutes depending on their size.
2. Prepare the Potatoes:
    - Drain the potatoes and let them cool slightly until they are cool enough to handle but still warm.
    - Peel the potatoes while they are still warm (this helps prevent the potatoes from becoming gummy) and pass them through a potato ricer or mash them until smooth. Spread the mashed potatoes on a clean work surface to cool completely, about 10-15 minutes.
3. Form the Gnocchi Dough:
    - Once the potatoes have cooled, mound them on a clean work surface and create a well in the center.
    - Sprinkle the flour over the potatoes and season with a pinch of salt.
    - Add the beaten egg to the center of the well.
4. Mix the Dough:
    - Using your hands, gradually incorporate the flour, potatoes, and egg until a soft dough forms. Be careful not to overwork the dough, as this can make the gnocchi dense.
5. Shape the Gnocchi:
    - Divide the dough into smaller sections.
    - Roll each section into a long rope about 1/2 inch (1 cm) thick.
    - Cut the ropes into 1-inch (2.5 cm) pieces. Optionally, you can roll each piece over the back of a fork to create ridges (this helps sauce cling to the gnocchi).
6. Cook the Gnocchi:
    - Bring a large pot of salted water to a boil.
    - Carefully drop the gnocchi into the boiling water, in batches if necessary to avoid overcrowding.
    - Cook until the gnocchi float to the surface, about 2-3 minutes. Remove them with a slotted spoon and transfer to a plate.
7. Serve:

- Serve the gnocchi immediately with your favorite sauce, such as marinara, pesto, or browned butter and sage.
- Garnish with grated Parmesan cheese and fresh herbs if desired.

Lidia Bastianich's gnocchi are light, pillowy, and full of potato flavor, perfect for a comforting and satisfying Italian meal. Enjoy these homemade gnocchi with family and friends, and savor the authentic taste of Italian cuisine!

Hugh Fearnley-Whittingstall - Roast Pork Belly

Ingredients:

- 2-3 pounds (about 1-1.5 kg) pork belly, skin-on
- Salt
- Freshly ground black pepper
- Optional: Fennel seeds, garlic, or herbs for additional flavor

Instructions:

1. Prep the Pork Belly:
    - Score the skin of the pork belly with a sharp knife, making cuts about 1/2 inch (1 cm) apart. Make sure to score through the skin and fat, but not into the meat.
2. Season the Pork Belly:
    - Rub salt generously all over the pork belly, making sure to get it into the cuts on the skin. Season with freshly ground black pepper and any additional optional seasonings like fennel seeds, garlic, or herbs.
3. Prepare for Roasting:
    - Place the pork belly, skin-side up, on a wire rack set over a roasting pan. This allows the air to circulate around the pork belly, helping the skin to crisp up.
4. Roast the Pork Belly:
    - Preheat your oven to 425°F (220°C).
    - Roast the pork belly in the preheated oven for 30 minutes to allow the skin to start crisping up.
5. Lower the Temperature:
    - After 30 minutes, reduce the oven temperature to 325°F (160°C) and continue roasting for another 1.5 to 2 hours, or until the pork belly is tender and cooked through. The internal temperature should reach 145°F (63°C) for safe consumption.
6. Crisp the Skin:
    - Increase the oven temperature to 425°F (220°C) again, or switch to the grill setting if your oven has one.
    - Roast or grill the pork belly for an additional 15-20 minutes, watching closely, until the skin is crispy and golden brown. Keep an eye on it to prevent burning.
7. Rest and Serve:
    - Remove the pork belly from the oven and let it rest for 10-15 minutes before slicing.
    - Slice the roast pork belly into thick slices and serve hot, with sides like roasted vegetables, applesauce, or a fresh salad.

Hugh Fearnley-Whittingstall's roast pork belly is a dish that's both simple and impressive, with its crispy crackling and tender meat. It's perfect for a comforting meal or a festive occasion. Enjoy the rich flavors and textures of this delicious roast!

Sanjeev Kapoor - Butter Chicken

Ingredients:

For the Marinade:

- 500g boneless, skinless chicken thighs or breasts, cut into bite-sized pieces
- 1/2 cup plain yogurt
- 1 tablespoon ginger-garlic paste (or finely minced ginger and garlic)
- 1 teaspoon Kashmiri red chili powder (or paprika for a milder flavor)
- 1/2 teaspoon ground turmeric
- 1 teaspoon garam masala
- 1 tablespoon lemon juice
- Salt, to taste

For the Butter Chicken Sauce:

- 2 tablespoons butter
- 1 tablespoon vegetable oil
- 1 large onion, finely chopped
- 2 teaspoons ginger-garlic paste
- 1 teaspoon Kashmiri red chili powder (adjust to taste)
- 1/2 teaspoon ground cumin
- 1/2 teaspoon ground coriander
- 1/2 teaspoon garam masala
- 1/4 teaspoon ground cardamom
- 1 cup tomato puree (passata)
- 1/2 cup heavy cream
- 1 tablespoon honey or sugar (optional, to balance acidity)
- Salt, to taste
- Fresh cilantro (coriander) leaves, chopped, for garnish

Instructions:

1. Marinate the Chicken:
    - In a bowl, combine the yogurt, ginger-garlic paste, Kashmiri red chili powder, turmeric, garam masala, lemon juice, and salt.
    - Add the chicken pieces to the marinade, ensuring they are well coated. Cover and refrigerate for at least 30 minutes, or up to 4 hours for best results.
2. Cook the Chicken:
    - Heat 1 tablespoon of butter and 1 tablespoon of vegetable oil in a large skillet or pan over medium-high heat.
    - Add the marinated chicken pieces, shaking off excess marinade. Cook until browned and cooked through, about 8-10 minutes. Remove the chicken from the pan and set aside.

3. Prepare the Butter Chicken Sauce:
    - In the same pan, add another tablespoon of butter. Add the finely chopped onion and cook until softened and translucent, about 5-7 minutes.
    - Add ginger-garlic paste and sauté for another minute until fragrant.
    - Stir in Kashmiri red chili powder, ground cumin, ground coriander, garam masala, and ground cardamom. Cook for a minute until spices are aromatic.
4. Simmer the Sauce:
    - Add the tomato puree (passata) to the pan. Bring to a gentle simmer and cook for 10-15 minutes, stirring occasionally, until the sauce thickens and the flavors meld together.
    - Stir in the heavy cream and honey or sugar (if using). Season with salt to taste.
5. Combine and Finish:
    - Add the cooked chicken pieces back to the pan. Simmer gently for another 5-7 minutes, allowing the chicken to absorb the flavors of the sauce.
    - Garnish with chopped fresh cilantro (coriander) leaves before serving.
6. Serve:
    - Serve hot Butter Chicken with steamed basmati rice or naan bread. Enjoy the creamy, flavorful dish!

Sanjeev Kapoor's Butter Chicken is a beloved Indian dish known for its creamy tomato sauce and tender chicken pieces. This simplified recipe captures the essence of traditional Indian flavors and is perfect for a comforting meal at home.

Cat Cora - Greek Salad

Ingredients:

- 2 large tomatoes, cut into wedges or chunks
- 1 cucumber, sliced (peeled if desired)
- 1 red onion, thinly sliced
- 1 green bell pepper, seeded and sliced
- 1/2 cup Kalamata olives, pitted
- 1/2 cup feta cheese, crumbled
- 1/4 cup extra virgin olive oil
- 2 tablespoons red wine vinegar
- 1 teaspoon dried oregano (or 1 tablespoon fresh oregano, chopped)
- Salt and freshly ground black pepper, to taste

Instructions:

1. Prepare the Vegetables:
    - In a large salad bowl, combine the tomato wedges, sliced cucumber, thinly sliced red onion, and sliced green bell pepper.
2. Add the Olives and Feta:
    - Add the Kalamata olives and crumbled feta cheese to the bowl with the vegetables.
3. Make the Dressing:
    - In a small bowl or jar, whisk together the extra virgin olive oil, red wine vinegar, dried oregano (or fresh oregano), salt, and pepper. Adjust seasoning to taste.
4. Assemble the Salad:
    - Drizzle the dressing over the salad ingredients in the bowl.
5. Toss Gently:
    - Gently toss the salad to combine all the ingredients and coat them evenly with the dressing.
6. Serve:
    - Serve the Greek Salad immediately as a side dish or a light main course.
    - Optionally, garnish with additional oregano leaves and a few whole Kalamata olives on top.

Cat Cora's Greek Salad is a colorful and flavorful dish that showcases the freshness of Mediterranean ingredients. It's perfect for any occasion, whether you're hosting a summer barbecue or looking for a healthy and satisfying meal option. Enjoy the crisp vegetables, tangy feta cheese, and briny olives in every bite!

Lorraine Pascale - Chocolate Brownies

Ingredients:

- 200g (7 oz) dark chocolate (around 70% cocoa solids), chopped
- 200g (7 oz) unsalted butter
- 250g (1 1/4 cups) caster sugar (superfine sugar)
- 3 large eggs
- 1 teaspoon vanilla extract
- 100g (3/4 cup) all-purpose flour (plain flour)
- 50g (1/2 cup) cocoa powder
- 1/2 teaspoon salt
- Optional: 100g (1/2 cup) chocolate chips or chopped nuts for extra texture

Instructions:

1. Preheat the Oven:
    - Preheat your oven to 180°C (350°F) or 160°C (320°F) fan. Grease and line a 20cm (8-inch) square baking tin with parchment paper, leaving some overhang for easy removal.
2. Melt the Chocolate and Butter:
    - In a heatproof bowl set over a pan of simmering water (double boiler method), melt the dark chocolate and unsalted butter together. Stir occasionally until smooth and well combined. Remove from heat and let it cool slightly.
3. Prepare the Brownie Batter:
    - In a large mixing bowl, whisk together the caster sugar, eggs, and vanilla extract until well combined and slightly frothy.
    - Gradually pour the melted chocolate mixture into the egg mixture, whisking continuously until smooth.
4. Add Dry Ingredients:
    - Sift in the all-purpose flour, cocoa powder, and salt into the chocolate mixture. Fold gently using a spatula until just combined. Be careful not to overmix.
    - Optionally, fold in chocolate chips or chopped nuts for added texture.
5. Bake the Brownies:
    - Pour the brownie batter into the prepared baking tin and smooth the top with a spatula.
    - Bake in the preheated oven for 25-30 minutes, or until a skewer inserted into the center comes out with a few moist crumbs attached. The brownies should be set around the edges but still slightly soft in the center.
6. Cool and Serve:
    - Remove the brownies from the oven and let them cool completely in the tin set on a wire rack.
    - Once cooled, lift the brownies out of the tin using the parchment paper overhang. Cut into squares or rectangles to serve.

7. Optional: Garnish:
    - Dust with cocoa powder or icing sugar before serving, if desired.

Lorraine Pascale's Chocolate Brownies are rich, fudgy, and perfect for satisfying chocolate cravings. They're great as a treat for gatherings, afternoon tea, or simply whenever you need a delicious pick-me-up. Enjoy these homemade brownies with a glass of milk or a scoop of vanilla ice cream for an extra special indulgence!

David Chang - Korean BBQ

Ingredients:

For the Marinade:

- 1/2 cup soy sauce
- 1/4 cup brown sugar
- 3 tablespoons rice wine (mirin) or dry white wine
- 2 tablespoons sesame oil
- 4 cloves garlic, minced
- 1 tablespoon grated ginger
- 2 green onions, finely chopped
- 1 teaspoon black pepper
- Optional: 1 tablespoon gochujang (Korean chili paste) for spiciness

For the BBQ:

- 1 1/2 pounds (700g) thinly sliced beef (such as ribeye, sirloin, or skirt steak)
- 1 pound (450g) thinly sliced pork belly
- Assorted vegetables for grilling (such as mushrooms, bell peppers, zucchini)
- Cooked white rice, for serving

Instructions:

1. Prepare the Marinade:
   - In a bowl, combine soy sauce, brown sugar, rice wine (or white wine), sesame oil, minced garlic, grated ginger, chopped green onions, black pepper, and gochujang (if using). Mix well until the sugar is dissolved.
2. Marinate the Meat:
   - Place the thinly sliced beef and pork belly in separate shallow dishes or resealable plastic bags.
   - Pour half of the marinade over the beef and the other half over the pork belly, ensuring all pieces are coated evenly. Marinate for at least 1 hour, or ideally overnight in the refrigerator for deeper flavor.
3. Prepare the Grill:
   - Preheat a grill or grill pan over medium-high heat. Make sure the grill is well-oiled to prevent sticking.
4. Grill the Meat and Vegetables:
   - Remove the marinated meat from the refrigerator and let it come to room temperature for about 15-20 minutes.
   - Grill the marinated beef and pork belly slices in batches, turning occasionally, until cooked to your desired doneness. Korean BBQ is typically cooked quickly, so each batch may take about 2-3 minutes per side depending on thickness.

- While grilling the meat, you can also grill assorted vegetables until tender and lightly charred.
5. **Serve:**
    - Transfer the grilled meat and vegetables to a serving platter.
    - Serve immediately with cooked white rice and any remaining marinade as a dipping sauce or drizzle over the meat.
    - Optionally, garnish with sesame seeds and additional chopped green onions for added flavor and presentation.

David Chang's Korean BBQ recipe emphasizes the bold flavors of the marinade and the interactive dining experience of grilling meats at the table. It's a delicious way to enjoy a taste of Korean cuisine with family and friends.

Jamie Oliver - Prawn Linguine

Ingredients:

- 300g linguine pasta
- 300g large raw prawns, peeled and deveined
- 2 cloves garlic, finely chopped
- 1 red chili, finely chopped (adjust amount to taste)
- Zest and juice of 1 lemon
- 1 tablespoon olive oil
- 2 tablespoons unsalted butter
- Salt and freshly ground black pepper, to taste
- Fresh parsley, chopped, for garnish

Instructions:

1. Cook the Linguine:
    - Bring a large pot of salted water to a boil. Cook the linguine according to package instructions until al dente. Reserve about 1/2 cup of pasta cooking water, then drain the pasta.
2. Prepare the Prawns:
    - While the pasta is cooking, heat the olive oil in a large skillet or frying pan over medium-high heat.
    - Add the chopped garlic and red chili to the pan. Sauté for about 1 minute until fragrant.
3. Cook the Prawns:
    - Add the prawns to the skillet. Cook for 2-3 minutes, stirring occasionally, until they turn pink and are just cooked through.
4. Combine the Pasta:
    - Add the drained linguine to the skillet with the prawns.
    - Add the butter, lemon zest, and lemon juice. Toss everything together gently until the pasta is coated evenly with the sauce. If the pasta seems dry, add a splash of the reserved pasta cooking water to loosen it up.
5. Season and Serve:
    - Season with salt and freshly ground black pepper to taste.
    - Sprinkle chopped fresh parsley over the pasta before serving for added freshness and color.
6. Serve Immediately:
    - Divide the prawn linguine among serving plates or bowls.
    - Optionally, garnish with additional lemon zest and parsley.

Jamie Oliver's Prawn Linguine is a quick and flavorful dish that's perfect for weeknight dinners or special occasions. The combination of garlic, chili, lemon, and butter creates a simple yet delicious sauce that complements the sweetness of the prawns beautifully. Enjoy this dish with a crisp green salad and a glass of white wine for a complete meal!

Marcus Wareing - Beef Wellington

Ingredients:

- 600g beef fillet, center-cut, trimmed of excess fat
- Salt and freshly ground black pepper
- 2 tablespoons olive oil
- 1 tablespoon Dijon mustard
- 200g mushrooms, finely chopped
- 2 cloves garlic, minced
- 1 tablespoon fresh thyme leaves, chopped
- 1 sheet puff pastry, thawed if frozen
- 1 egg, beaten (for egg wash)

Instructions:

1. Prepare the Beef:
   - Season the beef fillet generously with salt and pepper.
   - Heat the olive oil in a large skillet over high heat. Sear the beef fillet on all sides until browned, about 1-2 minutes per side. Remove from heat and let it cool slightly.
2. Coat with Mustard:
   - Brush the seared beef fillet all over with Dijon mustard. Set aside.
3. Prepare the Mushroom Duxelles:
   - In the same skillet, add a bit more olive oil if needed. Sauté the finely chopped mushrooms, garlic, and thyme over medium heat until the mushrooms release their moisture and become tender, about 5-7 minutes. Season with salt and pepper to taste. Remove from heat and let it cool.
4. Assemble the Wellington:
   - Roll out the puff pastry on a lightly floured surface into a rectangle large enough to wrap around the beef fillet completely.
   - Spread the mushroom duxelles evenly over the puff pastry, leaving a border around the edges.
   - Place the seared beef fillet on top of the mushroom duxelles.
5. Wrap and Seal:
   - Carefully wrap the puff pastry around the beef fillet, sealing the edges and trimming any excess pastry.
   - Brush the entire surface of the puff pastry with beaten egg to create a golden crust when baked.
6. Bake:
   - Preheat your oven to 200°C (400°F).
   - Place the Beef Wellington on a baking sheet lined with parchment paper.
   - Bake in the preheated oven for 25-30 minutes, or until the puff pastry is golden brown and cooked through, and the beef reaches your desired level of doneness

(for medium-rare, the internal temperature should be around 55-57°C or 130-135°F when measured with a meat thermometer).
7. **Rest and Serve:**
    - Remove the Beef Wellington from the oven and let it rest for 10 minutes before slicing.
    - Slice into thick portions and serve immediately, accompanied by your favorite sides like roasted vegetables or mashed potatoes.

Marcus Wareing's Beef Wellington is a show-stopping dish that combines tender beef fillet with savory mushroom duxelles, all wrapped in a flaky puff pastry crust. While it requires some effort, it's perfect for special occasions when you want to impress your guests with a gourmet meal at home. Enjoy the rich flavors and textures of this classic dish!

Yotam Ottolenghi - Shakshuka

Ingredients:

- 2 tablespoons olive oil
- 1 onion, finely chopped
- 1 red bell pepper, seeded and chopped
- 1 yellow bell pepper, seeded and chopped
- 3 cloves garlic, minced
- 1 teaspoon ground cumin
- 1 teaspoon smoked paprika
- 1/2 teaspoon chili flakes (adjust to taste)
- 1 teaspoon ground coriander (optional)
- 800g (28 oz) canned diced tomatoes
- Salt and freshly ground black pepper, to taste
- 4-6 large eggs
- Fresh parsley or cilantro (coriander), chopped, for garnish
- Crusty bread or pita, for serving

Instructions:

1. Sauté the Vegetables:
   - Heat olive oil in a large skillet or frying pan over medium heat. Add the chopped onion and bell peppers. Sauté for about 5-7 minutes, or until the vegetables are softened and slightly caramelized.
2. Add the Spices:
   - Add the minced garlic, ground cumin, smoked paprika, chili flakes, and ground coriander (if using). Cook for 1-2 minutes, stirring constantly, until fragrant.
3. Simmer the Tomato Sauce:
   - Pour in the canned diced tomatoes (including juices) into the skillet. Season with salt and pepper to taste. Bring the mixture to a simmer and cook for 10-15 minutes, stirring occasionally, until the sauce has thickened slightly.
4. Poach the Eggs:
   - Using a spoon, create small indentations (or "wells") in the tomato and pepper mixture for each egg.
   - Crack each egg into a small bowl, then carefully slide each egg into its own indentation in the tomato mixture.
   - Cover the skillet with a lid or aluminum foil. Cook for 5-7 minutes, or until the egg whites are set but the yolks are still runny (cook longer if you prefer firmer yolks).
5. Serve:
   - Remove the skillet from heat. Sprinkle chopped fresh parsley or cilantro over the shakshuka.
   - Serve hot directly from the skillet, with crusty bread or pita on the side for dipping and scooping up the delicious tomato sauce and eggs.

Yotam Ottolenghi's Shakshuka is a comforting and satisfying dish that's perfect for brunch or any meal of the day. The combination of spices, tomatoes, peppers, and eggs creates a flavorful and hearty experience that's sure to become a favorite. Enjoy the rich, savory flavors with your favorite bread for a complete meal!

Eric Ripert - Bouillabaisse

Ingredients:

- 500g mixed firm white fish fillets (such as cod, haddock, or halibut), cut into chunks
- 300g mixed shellfish (such as mussels, clams, and shrimp), cleaned and scrubbed
- 1 onion, finely chopped
- 2 cloves garlic, minced
- 1 fennel bulb, thinly sliced
- 1 leek, white and light green parts only, thinly sliced
- 1 carrot, peeled and thinly sliced
- 1 celery stalk, thinly sliced
- 1 red bell pepper, seeded and thinly sliced
- 1 yellow bell pepper, seeded and thinly sliced
- 1 bay leaf
- 1 sprig fresh thyme
- 1 teaspoon saffron threads (optional)
- 400g canned diced tomatoes
- 750ml (3 cups) fish or seafood stock
- 250ml (1 cup) dry white wine
- 2 tablespoons olive oil
- Salt and freshly ground black pepper, to taste
- Fresh parsley, chopped, for garnish
- Crusty bread, for serving

Instructions:

1. Prepare the Vegetables:
   - Heat olive oil in a large pot or Dutch oven over medium heat. Add the chopped onion, minced garlic, sliced fennel, leek, carrot, celery, and bell peppers. Sauté for 8-10 minutes until vegetables are softened.
2. Add Aromatics and Liquids:
   - Stir in the bay leaf, thyme sprig, and saffron threads (if using). Cook for another minute until fragrant.
   - Pour in the canned diced tomatoes, fish or seafood stock, and dry white wine. Season with salt and pepper to taste. Bring to a simmer and cook for 15-20 minutes, allowing the flavors to meld together.
3. Cook the Seafood:
   - Add the mixed fish fillets to the simmering broth. Cook for 3-5 minutes, until the fish is just cooked through and opaque.
   - Add the cleaned shellfish (mussels, clams, shrimp) to the pot. Cover with a lid and cook for an additional 5-7 minutes, or until the shellfish have opened (discard any that do not open).
4. Serve:

- Remove the pot from heat. Discard the bay leaf and thyme sprig.
- Ladle the bouillabaisse into serving bowls, making sure to distribute the seafood and vegetables evenly.
- Garnish with chopped fresh parsley.
- Serve hot with crusty bread for dipping into the flavorful broth.

Eric Ripert's Bouillabaisse is a comforting and elegant dish that highlights the natural flavors of seafood with a fragrant and aromatic broth. Enjoy this hearty stew as a main course for a special occasion or a gathering with friends and family.

Gail Simmons - Apple Pie

Ingredients:

For the Pie Crust:

- 2 1/2 cups all-purpose flour
- 1 tablespoon granulated sugar
- 1 teaspoon salt
- 1 cup (2 sticks) unsalted butter, cold and cut into cubes
- 6-8 tablespoons ice water

For the Apple Filling:

- 6-7 medium-sized apples (such as Granny Smith or Honeycrisp), peeled, cored, and sliced thinly
- 1/2 cup granulated sugar
- 1/4 cup packed light brown sugar
- 1 teaspoon ground cinnamon
- 1/4 teaspoon ground nutmeg
- 1/4 teaspoon ground cloves
- 1/4 teaspoon salt
- 1 tablespoon lemon juice
- 2 tablespoons unsalted butter, cut into small pieces

For Assembly:

- 1 egg, beaten (for egg wash)
- 1 tablespoon granulated sugar (for sprinkling)

Instructions:

1. Make the Pie Crust:
    - In a large mixing bowl, combine the flour, sugar, and salt. Add the cold cubed butter.
    - Use a pastry cutter or your fingertips to work the butter into the flour mixture until it resembles coarse crumbs.
    - Gradually add ice water, one tablespoon at a time, mixing with a fork until the dough just begins to come together.
    - Divide the dough in half, form into two discs, wrap each disc in plastic wrap, and refrigerate for at least 1 hour.
2. Prepare the Apple Filling:
    - In a large bowl, combine the sliced apples, granulated sugar, brown sugar, cinnamon, nutmeg, cloves, salt, and lemon juice. Toss until the apples are evenly coated.

3. Assemble the Pie:
   - Preheat your oven to 220°C (425°F).
   - On a lightly floured surface, roll out one disc of chilled pie dough into a circle large enough to fit a 9-inch pie dish. Transfer the dough to the pie dish, gently pressing it into the bottom and sides.
4. Fill the Pie:
   - Pour the apple filling into the prepared pie crust, mounding it slightly in the center. Dot the top with small pieces of butter.
5. Top and Seal the Pie:
   - Roll out the second disc of chilled pie dough into a circle. Place it over the apple filling.
   - Trim any excess dough from the edges, leaving about a 1-inch overhang. Fold the overhang under itself and crimp the edges to seal. Cut a few small slits in the top crust to allow steam to escape.
6. Bake the Pie:
   - Brush the top crust with beaten egg and sprinkle with granulated sugar.
   - Place the pie on a baking sheet (to catch any drips) and bake in the preheated oven for 45-55 minutes, or until the crust is golden brown and the filling is bubbling.
   - If the edges of the crust start to brown too quickly, cover them with foil or a pie shield halfway through baking.
7. Cool and Serve:
   - Remove the pie from the oven and let it cool on a wire rack for at least 2 hours before slicing and serving.
   - Serve warm or at room temperature, optionally with a scoop of vanilla ice cream or a dollop of whipped cream.

Gail Simmons' Apple Pie is a comforting dessert that showcases the sweetness of apples with warm spices, encased in a flaky, buttery crust. It's perfect for any occasion, from family gatherings to holiday celebrations. Enjoy the aroma of baked apples and cinnamon filling your kitchen as you bake this delicious pie!

Dominique Ansel - Cronuts

Ingredients:

For the Dough:

- 1 package (7g) active dry yeast
- 1/4 cup (60ml) warm water (around 110°F/45°C)
- 1/4 cup (50g) granulated sugar
- 1 teaspoon salt
- 1 cup (240ml) whole milk, warmed
- 2 1/2 cups (315g) all-purpose flour, plus extra for dusting
- 1 cup (2 sticks, 225g) unsalted butter, cold
- Vegetable oil, for frying

For the Glaze:

- 1 1/2 cups (180g) powdered sugar
- 2-3 tablespoons milk or water
- 1 teaspoon vanilla extract (optional)

Instructions:

1. Prepare the Dough:
   - In a small bowl, dissolve the yeast in warm water with a pinch of sugar. Let it sit for about 5 minutes until frothy.
   - In a large mixing bowl or the bowl of a stand mixer fitted with a dough hook, combine the remaining sugar, salt, warmed milk, and yeast mixture.
   - Gradually add the flour, mixing until a soft dough forms.
2. Incorporate the Butter:
   - Cut the cold butter into small cubes and toss them in a little flour to coat.
   - On a lightly floured surface, roll out the dough into a rectangle about 1/2 inch thick.
   - Scatter half of the butter cubes over the center third of the dough. Fold one side over the butter, then fold the other side over the top, like folding a letter.
   - Roll out the dough again into a rectangle and repeat the folding process with the remaining butter cubes.
3. Chill the Dough:
   - Wrap the dough in plastic wrap and refrigerate for at least 1 hour, or overnight if possible. This allows the dough to rest and the layers to develop.
4. Shape and Fry the Cronuts:
   - On a lightly floured surface, roll out the chilled dough to about 1/2 inch thick.
   - Using a 3-inch round cutter, cut out circles of dough. Use a smaller cutter to make a hole in the center of each circle, creating the classic donut shape.

- Place the shaped cronuts on a baking sheet lined with parchment paper and let them rise for about 30-45 minutes, until slightly puffed.
5. **Fry the Cronuts:**
    - Heat vegetable oil in a deep fryer or large pot to 350°F (180°C).
    - Carefully place the cronuts into the hot oil, a few at a time, and fry for about 2-3 minutes per side, until golden brown and puffed.
    - Remove the cronuts from the oil using a slotted spoon and drain on a paper towel-lined plate.
6. **Glaze the Cronuts:**
    - In a bowl, whisk together powdered sugar, milk or water, and vanilla extract (if using) until smooth. Adjust the consistency by adding more milk or water as needed.
    - Dip each cronut into the glaze while still warm. Allow excess glaze to drip off before transferring to a wire rack to set.
7. **Serve and Enjoy:**
    - Serve the cronuts warm or at room temperature. Enjoy the flaky layers and sweet glaze of your homemade cronuts inspired by Dominique Ansel's original creation!

Dominique Ansel's Cronuts are a delightful treat that blend the best aspects of croissants and donuts, making them a popular choice among pastry enthusiasts worldwide. This simplified version allows you to recreate a taste of this famous pastry at home!

Carla Hall - Fried Chicken

Ingredients:

- 1 whole chicken, cut into pieces (or use your preferred chicken parts)
- 2 cups buttermilk
- 2 cups all-purpose flour
- 1 tablespoon salt
- 1 tablespoon black pepper
- 1 teaspoon paprika
- 1 teaspoon garlic powder
- 1 teaspoon onion powder
- Vegetable oil, for frying

Instructions:

1. Marinate the Chicken:
    - Place the chicken pieces in a large bowl and cover them with buttermilk. Ensure all pieces are coated. Marinate in the refrigerator for at least 1 hour, or preferably overnight for more flavor.
2. Prepare the Coating:
    - In a shallow dish or bowl, mix together the flour, salt, black pepper, paprika, garlic powder, and onion powder.
3. Coat the Chicken:
    - Remove each piece of chicken from the buttermilk, allowing excess to drip off.
    - Dredge the chicken pieces in the seasoned flour mixture, coating them evenly. Press the flour onto the chicken to ensure a good coating.
4. Fry the Chicken:
    - Heat vegetable oil in a large, heavy-bottomed pot or deep fryer to 350°F (175°C).
    - Carefully place a few chicken pieces in the hot oil, skin-side down. Fry in batches to avoid crowding the pot, which can lower the oil temperature.
    - Fry the chicken for about 15-20 minutes, turning occasionally, until golden brown and cooked through. The internal temperature should reach 165°F (74°C) for the chicken to be fully cooked.
5. Drain and Serve:
    - Remove the fried chicken from the oil using tongs or a slotted spoon. Place them on a wire rack or paper towels to drain excess oil.
    - Allow the fried chicken to rest for a few minutes before serving to let the juices settle.
6. Enjoy:
    - Serve the crispy fried chicken hot, optionally with your favorite sides such as mashed potatoes, coleslaw, biscuits, or cornbread.

Carla Hall's Fried Chicken is a comforting and classic dish that's perfect for a family meal or gathering. The buttermilk marinade ensures tender and juicy chicken, while the seasoned flour coating gives it a deliciously crispy crust. Enjoy the homemade goodness of this Southern-inspired favorite!

Julia Child - Coq au Vin

Ingredients:

- 1 whole chicken, cut into 8 pieces (or use chicken thighs and drumsticks)
- Salt and freshly ground black pepper, to taste
- 4 slices thick-cut bacon, diced
- 2 tablespoons olive oil
- 1 onion, finely chopped
- 2 carrots, peeled and sliced
- 2 cloves garlic, minced
- 250g (about 8 oz) mushrooms, quartered
- 2 tablespoons all-purpose flour
- 750ml (3 cups) red wine (such as Burgundy or Pinot Noir)
- 250ml (1 cup) chicken broth
- 2 tablespoons tomato paste
- 1 bouquet garni (bundle of herbs such as thyme, parsley, and bay leaf, tied together)
- Fresh parsley, chopped, for garnish

Instructions:

1. **Season and Brown the Chicken:**
    - Season the chicken pieces generously with salt and pepper.
    - In a large Dutch oven or heavy-bottomed pot, cook the diced bacon over medium heat until crisp. Remove the bacon with a slotted spoon and set aside.
    - Add olive oil to the pot. Working in batches if necessary, brown the chicken pieces on all sides. Remove the chicken and set aside.
2. **Sauté the Vegetables:**
    - In the same pot, add the chopped onion and sliced carrots. Cook for about 5 minutes until softened.
    - Add the minced garlic and quartered mushrooms. Cook for another 3-4 minutes until the mushrooms begin to brown.
3. **Make the Sauce:**
    - Sprinkle the flour over the vegetables in the pot. Stir well to combine and cook for 1-2 minutes to remove the raw flour taste.
    - Gradually pour in the red wine and chicken broth, stirring constantly to incorporate any browned bits from the bottom of the pot.
    - Stir in the tomato paste until dissolved. Add the bouquet garni and return the bacon and chicken pieces to the pot, along with any accumulated juices.
4. **Simmer and Cook:**
    - Bring the mixture to a simmer. Reduce the heat to low, cover, and simmer gently for 1 to 1.5 hours, or until the chicken is tender and cooked through. Stir occasionally.
5. **Serve:**

- Remove the bouquet garni and discard.
- Taste and adjust seasoning with salt and pepper if needed.
- Serve the Coq au Vin hot, garnished with chopped fresh parsley.

Julia Child's Coq au Vin is traditionally served with mashed potatoes, rice, or crusty bread to soak up the delicious sauce. This simplified version captures the essence of this classic French dish, perfect for a special dinner at home. Enjoy the robust flavors and tender chicken in a dish that epitomizes comfort and elegance!

Wolfgang Puck - Pumpkin Soup

Ingredients:

- 1 tablespoon olive oil
- 1 onion, chopped
- 2 cloves garlic, minced
- 1 teaspoon ground cinnamon
- 1/2 teaspoon ground nutmeg
- 1/4 teaspoon ground cloves
- 1/4 teaspoon ground ginger
- 1/4 teaspoon ground allspice (optional)
- 750g (about 1 1/2 pounds) pumpkin or butternut squash, peeled, seeded, and diced (about 4 cups)
- 4 cups vegetable or chicken broth
- 1 cup coconut milk or heavy cream
- Salt and freshly ground black pepper, to taste
- Pumpkin seeds, toasted (for garnish, optional)
- Fresh parsley or chives, chopped (for garnish, optional)

Instructions:

1. Sauté the Aromatics:
    - In a large pot or Dutch oven, heat olive oil over medium heat. Add the chopped onion and sauté until softened and translucent, about 5-7 minutes.
    - Add the minced garlic, ground cinnamon, nutmeg, cloves, ginger, and allspice (if using). Cook for another 1-2 minutes until fragrant.
2. Cook the Pumpkin:
    - Add the diced pumpkin or butternut squash to the pot. Stir to combine with the aromatics.
    - Pour in the vegetable or chicken broth, ensuring the pumpkin is covered. Bring to a boil, then reduce the heat to low. Simmer uncovered for 15-20 minutes, or until the pumpkin is tender and easily pierced with a fork.
3. Blend the Soup:
    - Remove the pot from heat. Using an immersion blender, blend the soup until smooth and creamy. Alternatively, carefully transfer the soup in batches to a blender and blend until smooth, then return to the pot.
4. Add Cream and Seasoning:
    - Stir in the coconut milk or heavy cream until well combined. Season with salt and pepper to taste. Adjust the consistency with additional broth or water if desired.
5. Serve:
    - Ladle the pumpkin soup into bowls. Garnish each serving with toasted pumpkin seeds and chopped parsley or chives if desired.
    - Serve hot, optionally with crusty bread or rolls on the side.

Wolfgang Puck's Pumpkin Soup is a comforting and flavorful dish that celebrates the natural sweetness of pumpkin with warm spices. It's perfect for a cozy meal during cooler months or as an elegant starter for a special dinner. Enjoy the creamy texture and rich flavors of this delicious soup!

Ina Garten - Lemon Roast Chicken

Ingredients:

- 1 whole chicken (about 4-5 pounds)
- 2 lemons
- 4 cloves garlic, minced
- 2 tablespoons olive oil
- 1 teaspoon dried thyme (or 1 tablespoon fresh thyme leaves)
- Salt and freshly ground black pepper, to taste
- Fresh herbs (such as thyme, rosemary, or parsley), for garnish (optional)

Instructions:

1. Preheat the Oven:
    - Preheat your oven to 425°F (220°C).
2. Prepare the Chicken:
    - Rinse the chicken inside and out under cold running water. Pat dry with paper towels.
    - Zest one of the lemons and set the zest aside. Cut both lemons in half.
3. Season the Chicken:
    - In a small bowl, combine the minced garlic, olive oil, dried thyme (if using fresh thyme, add it later), and lemon zest. Mix well to create a paste.
    - Rub the garlic and lemon mixture all over the chicken, including under the skin if possible. Season generously with salt and pepper, inside and out.
    - Place the used lemon halves inside the cavity of the chicken.
4. Roast the Chicken:
    - Place the chicken breast-side up on a roasting pan or baking dish with a rack. Tuck the wing tips under the body of the chicken.
    - If using fresh thyme, sprinkle it over the chicken.
    - Roast the chicken in the preheated oven for about 1 hour to 1 hour 15 minutes, or until the juices run clear when you cut between a leg and thigh.
    - Optional: Halfway through roasting, baste the chicken with pan juices or additional olive oil if desired.
5. Rest and Serve:
    - Remove the chicken from the oven and let it rest for 10-15 minutes before carving.
    - Garnish with fresh herbs if desired.
    - Serve the lemon roast chicken hot, with your favorite sides such as roasted vegetables, mashed potatoes, or a green salad.

Ina Garten's Lemon Roast Chicken is a flavorful and comforting dish that's perfect for a family dinner or entertaining guests. The combination of garlic, lemon, and thyme infuses the chicken with delicious aromas and enhances its natural flavors. Enjoy the juicy and tender meat with a hint of citrus zest in every bite!